Much Ado About Nothing

WILLIAM SHAKESPEARE

Guide written by

Lorna Syred

A *Letts* Literature Guide

First published 1997

Letts Educational
Aldine House
Aldine Place
London W12 8AW
0181 740 2266

Text © Lorna Syred 1997

Typeset by Jordan Publishing Design

Text design Jonathan Barnard

Cover and text illustrations Hugh Marshall

Graphic illustration Hugh Marshall

Design © BPP (Letts Educational) Ltd

British Library Cataloguing in Publication Data
A CIP record for this book is available from the British Library

ISBN 1 85758 491 0

Printed and bound in Great Britain
by Nuffield Press, Abingdon

Letts Educational is the trading name of BPP (Letts Educational) Ltd

Contents

Plot synopsis   4

Who's who in *Much Ado About Nothing*   8

Themes and images in *Much Ado About Nothing*   19

Text commentary Act One   24

Self-test questions Act One   29

Text commentary Act Two   31

Self-test questions Act Two   36

Text commentary Act Three   37

Self-test questions Act Three   43

Text commentary Act Four   44

Self-test questions Act Four   47

Text commentary Act Five   49

Self-test questions Act Five   52

Self-test answers   54

Writing an examination essay   61

Plot synopsis

A note on structure: *Much Ado About Nothing* is constructed from two plots which complement and feed off each other, but have basically separate storylines. In some ways they are in opposition to each other: one concerns a plan to build a relationship, through trickery and deception; the other concerns a plan to destroy a relationship, through the same means. To simplify matters, it helps to look at the plots individually, but you must remember that they are concurrent with each other, and that the main characters play an important role in *both* plots.

Hero/Claudio plot: This is the more dramatic of the two plots, providing tension and suspense. It leads the play to the edges of a conventional tragedy. Don Pedro, Prince of Arragon, returns from the wars, bringing with him Claudio, a young count from Florence. Claudio falls in love with Hero, daughter of the Governor of Messina.

Don John, the Prince's evil and jealous illegitimate brother, plots to destroy the romance, vowing to cross any friend of Don Pedro's. His first plot fails, but he is determined to continue attempting to wreck the proposed marriage. He enthusiastically agrees to Borachio's plan to make Hero look as if she has been unfaithful to Claudio.

Claudio and Don Pedro are convinced by the trick and believe Hero to be disloyal and corrupt. On the day of their wedding, Claudio refuses to marry Hero. As Hero protests her innocence and faints, Claudio and his followers leave her for dead. The friar comes up with a plan to save Hero's reputation: her family are to announce that she is dead, until the mystery can be solved.

Meanwhile, Dogberry, the village constable, and his partner Verges, have uncovered the evil plot, but they are so idiotic and incompetent that Leonato will not stop to listen to them. They do, eventually, bring the villains to him and the truth is discovered.

Claudio is distraught. He asks Leonato to choose his revenge. Claudio's 'punishment' is to marry Leonato's niece. At the wedding, the bride removes a mask to reveal the original bride, Hero. Claudio is overcome with happiness and relief.

Beatrice/Benedick plot: This is the more humorous of the two plots, and, to some, the most appealing. It is not given as much stage time as the other plot, nor does it provide the 'climax' to the play. The characters, however, often dominate our attention.

Beatrice is an orphan who is under the guardianship of Leonato. Benedick is a visiting soldier, who has obviously stayed in Messina before. The long-running feud between these two soon becomes apparent to the audience. We are never really given the reasons behind this feud, although there is a suggestion that they once had a brief flirtation. We are also able to guess at a possible secret attraction between them. The quick and witty repartee of Beatrice and Benedick amuses the other characters and, of course, the audience. Much humour is derived from the realisation that, although sworn enemies, they have much in common. They both have a sharp and deadly wit and a carefree attitude to life. Both profess their repulsion for the idea of marriage.

Don Pedro plans to trick the two into falling in love with each other. He and his friends pretend that Beatrice is passionately in love with Benedick, by allowing him to overhear their conversation on the topic. The intention is that Benedick will soften and want to return Beatrice's love. Hero, Beatrice's cousin, then does exactly the same, ensuring that Beatrice overhears her conversation about Benedick's unrequited love for her. The trick works, and the couple reluctantly allow themselves to fall in love.

Both plots end happily. Don John is captured and Hero and Claudio are reconciled. Beatrice and Benedick accept their love for one another and are brought together. The play ends with the prospect of two weddings.

Pairs – symmetry of structure

Much Ado About Nothing is a play constructed from pairs of plots, ideas and characters which contrast and complement each other.

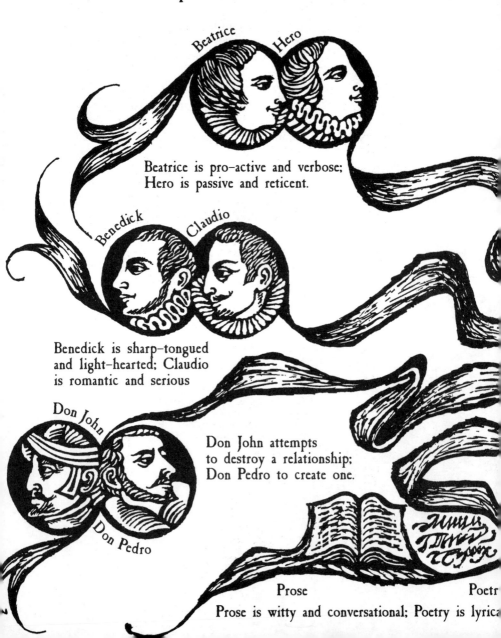

Beatrice is pro-active and verbose; Hero is passive and reticent.

Benedick is sharp-tongued and light-hearted; Claudio is romantic and serious

Don John attempts to destroy a relationship; Don Pedro to create one.

Prose is witty and conversational; Poetry is lyrica

The Hero/Claudio plot aims to destroy a relationship; the Beatrice/Benedick plot aims to build a relationship.

Beatrice

Beatrice

Beatrice's role in her society is one that allows her to go beyond the boundaries of conventional female behaviour. Unlike Hero, she has no parents to be 'dutiful' towards, although she does have the acceptance of those high in Messina society. Her position is an insecure one, however. She is not heir to any of Leonato's fortune and will have to survive on her own merits. This lack of close family or obligation adds to Beatrice's presentation as a 'free spirit'. She prides herself on her independence from the conventions of love and courtship and is able to banter and exchange jokes and insults with male company in a way that would be forbidden to Hero. She understands the differences between her position and Hero's when she says 'Yes, faith; it is my cousin's duty to make curtsy and say, "Father as it please you" (after an onslaught against the idea of marriage) 'Just, if he send me no husband; for the which blessing I am at him upon my knees every morning and evening'. Marriage is what the 'ordinary' Hero can expect, but is not for the likes of Beatrice. Despite her sharp tongue and independent spirit, we see a fierce loyalty to her cousin which puts some of the other characters to shame, and a kindness and consideration for her family and friends.

Everyone in *Much Ado About Nothing* wears a mask, at some point, to cover their real intentions or feelings. Beatrice's mask is that of self-deception. You will have to decide for yourself how far this interpretation can stretch: to what extent was her attraction to Benedick present *before* her sudden 'revelation'? Look closely at her behaviour in Act 1 when she is eager to receive news of her enemy, and insists on reinstating their feud: 'I wonder that you still be talking Signor Benedick – nobody marks you' – and in Act 2 when she alludes to a former flirtation: '...I gave him use for it, a double heart for his single one'. Or perhaps her 'mask' is only taken away with the sudden realisation of her own shortcomings, which are so readily pointed out by her cousin. 'Stand I condemned for pride and scorn so much?/Contempt, farewell! and maiden pride, adieu!' At the very least, the self-deception which is obvious to the audience is Beatrice's inability to see her own likeness to Benedick – for they surely are the male and female counterparts of each other.

Another issue surrounding the character of Beatrice is that of how well she fares from the conclusion of the play. We first meet her as a fiery, independent-minded woman, able to terrify men into 'keeping friends' with her. Her 'transformation' might seem to relegate her to the ranks of the 'ordinary'. How far has she simply compromised her original principles and allowed herself to be 'tamed', like Kate in *The Taming of the Shrew*? She even seems to acknowledge this herself, at one point, when she resolves that she will be 'Taming my wild heart to thy loving hand!' How significant is Benedick's cry of 'Peace! I will stop your mouth!' at the end of the play? Or has Beatrice simply found her equal in Benedick – someone who will match her sharpness of wit but allow her to remain true to herself and exist outside the conventions of feminine behaviour?

In terms of a feminist critique, it is also worth looking at the the scene where Beatrice demands that Benedick kill Claudio in order to prove his love for her. She rails against the conventions of courtiers and the frivolous tastes and fashions of men of the day. 'But manhood is melted into curtsies, valour into compliment, and men are only turned into tongue, and trim ones too!' We see here Beatrice's frustrations with her role of 'woman' in society, and her angry acceptance that there are some conventions by which she must abide. She cannot challenge Claudio herself; she must send a man to do it. At this point she clearly feels defeated by her own position: 'I cannot be a man with wishing, therefore I will die a woman with grieving.'

There are many different ways of looking at the character of Beatrice. At her simplest she has simply been wearing a 'mask' which covered her true feelings for her 'enemy'. Whichever way you choose to view Beatrice, she is certainly one of the most appealing and entertaining characters in the play.

Benedick

Benedick

Benedick, as mentioned on page 9, is Beatrice's male counterpart, and therefore many of the same issues and arguments surround him. He too wears a 'mask', which is removed when he hears of Beatrice's supposed devotion and of his own shortcomings. And, like Beatrice, he makes a big fuss about his distaste for the idea of marriage and he holds Claudio in contempt for his easy conversion to it. Like Beatrice, there are clues that Benedick is attracted to her, but they are hidden, even to himself. For example, his comment to Claudio, comparing Hero unfavourably with her- '…there's her cousin, an' were she not possessed with a fury, exceeds her as much in beauty as the first of May doth the last of December.' Look also at Benedick's distress at Beatrice's insultingly low opinion of him in the masque scene – 'O, she misused me past the endurance of a block!' – and the way he instantly thinks in terms of marriage – 'I would not marry her, though she were endowed with all that Adam left him before he transgressed'.

Benedick also shares characteristics with Beatrice in his flouting of the conventions and 'norms' of his position in society. He shuns the formal conventions of courtship that Claudio slavishly follows, mocking some of the ways of the court and his duty towards the prince: for example, his joking use of the usually solemn vow 'On my allegiance' and his wildly exaggerated plea for the prince to command him to go on an errand so that he can avoid Beatrice. There is an unfortunate irony in his behaviour here, for the court jester had leave to flout conventions in this manner in order to amuse the royal household. Beatrice's insulting comment about his role as 'the Prince's jester' could, then, have been painfully near the truth. Benedick does have a brief conversion to the 'romantic courtier', however. Act 3, scene 2 shows him changed in appearance as well as behaviour. He appears to have altered his manner of dress, shaved his beard and started using perfume. Some performances have made his new 'image' an exaggerated and cumbersome version of the courtier's costume of the time. This is to show that he is trying (and failing) to follow the fashion of courtly love. His new image does not last long, however, and in Act 5 we see him dropping this new 'mask' with an acceptance that he '…cannot woo in festival terms'.

Benedick is presented to us first through report. There are conflicting accounts: the Messenger says that he has heard nothing but good of Benedick, but Beatrice tells us that he is inconstant in friendship and not worthy of honour on the battlefield. We also learn of the 'merry war' between him and Beatrice and suspect that she may be prejudiced in her views. Our curiosity, then, has been aroused before we actually encounter Benedick. When we do, we note that it is Beatrice who takes the aggressive initiative, and Benedick who closes the battle, rather than pursue it further: 'But keep your way a' God's name, I have done'. Even when Benedick does initiate an attack, under cover of his mask, it is instantly squashed by Beatrice's onslaught of retaliation. Does either Benedick or Beatrice have the upper hand in their relationship? Or is it truly a meeting of equals?

Hero

Hero

Hero stands in contrast to Beatrice in the play. Whilst Beatrice can live outside the conventions of society, Hero must live within them, under the auspices of her father.

In the opening scene of the play, the contrast is striking. Beatrice's outstanding feature is her verbosity and wit; Hero's is her silence. She says nothing at all, in fact, until after Act 1, although she is present for most of the action. This silence emphasises the boundaries set by Hero's society – she is surrounded by her father and four young men with whom she is not well acquainted, so it is not for her to speak.

Her courtship is of a different type to Beatrice's. It is public, and played out through the normal forum of courtly love. Hero and Claudio's love is based purely on visual encounter and Hero is wooed by proxy by an older and more experienced man. Leonato's blessing is sought, and he literally 'gives' Hero to Claudio, along with his fortune. We never actually hear Hero's side of the story,but are left to wonder whether she would have been just as happy had it really been Don Pedro who wished to marry her. She seems content to accept the way things are, in stark contrast to Beatrice and her ravings against the constraints of womanhood.

There is a little more to Hero than an obedient simpleton, however. She is passive and dutiful, but we see a playful and humorous side to her nature when she is able to drop her 'mask'. She banters with Don Pedro at the Masque Ball and exchanges quips with Margaret and Beatrice whilst preparing for her wedding – although her talk is limited to that of fashion and costume, as if she is preparing herself for a 'role'. The part she plays in the deception of Beatrice is another 'role'. She speaks with exaggerated theatricality, using verse and figurative language. This is as if to heighten the audience's awareness of the 'stage-play' nature of the deception. She seems fairly eager to point out Beatrice's shortcomings, however, and one suspects that she has been longing to do this for some time, and can only do so now under cover of her 'role'.

Hero's behaviour at her wedding is in keeping with the rest of her characterisation: she makes a gentle attempt to stand up for herself and then swoons, unable to cope with her situation. She defends herself once again to the Friar, and then appears to agree passively to his plan: she is not asked her opinion. She is not represented as having a particular opinion about her 'second' marriage to Claudio, but fulfils her duty: to her father and to the man she had been given to in marriage.

Hero is the most constant character in the play – in several ways. She is unswerving in her acceptance of duty, and remains loyal to her fiancee, even when he has deserted her and accused her of being all that she is not: corrupt and unfaithful. Her characterisation, although undeveloped, is consistent: she is a dutiful daughter, successfully conditioned into accepting the rules of society.

Claudio

Claudio

As Hero stands in opposition to Beatrice, so Claudio stands in opposition to Benedick. He is the romantic lover of the play, his lyrical verse contrasting strongly with Benedick's strident prose. His courtship of Hero follows all the codes and customs of the time. He has some attributes of a tragic hero: he is well respected, and therefore has a long way to fall. He also has what might be termed 'tragic flaws': he is gullible, and, like Othello, he misplaces his trust. His gullibility is exposed early on. He is unable to judge whether Benedick takes him seriously as a lover: 'Thou thinkest I am in sport' and perhaps unwise in enlisting his opinion in the first place. He is easily gulled by Don John at the Masque, and then too easily believes what Benedick tells him: 'The Prince hath got your Hero'. This tendency to believe, somewhat naively, in false appearances sets up our expectations for his ready acceptance of Hero's infidelity, his misplaced trust in Don John, and also his acceptance of Leonato's trick at the end of the play. These flaws cause his downfall because they are exposed to the maliciousness of Don John.

The play is not a tragedy, however, and so Claudio is not quite a tragic figure. He does not have the complexity of characterisation of a hero figure, neither does he show any signs of nobility of spirit. In fact, the only signs of Claudio's bravery are given to us by report, at the opening of the play – 'He hath bourne himself beyond the promise of his age, doing, in the figure of a lamb, the feats of a lion'. He is not capable of the same feats off the battlefield, however, for he has to have someone else woo his woman for him, and seems ready to believe any idea that is put in front of him. He also has some distasteful aspects to his character: he too easily discards Hero, and does not, initially, 'mourn' her in the way that the Friar predicts, bouncing back easily from news of her death. It is as if the depth of his love extends no further than what he can see with his eyes, both in terms of Hero's beauty and in terms of what version of the truth he is presented with. This is made clear in his response to the knowledge that Hero was innocent all along – 'Sweet Hero, now your image doth appear/In the rare semblance that I loved it first'. His distress at Hero's supposed infidelity seems to come not so much from the betrayal of the person he most trusts, but from feeling that her *beauty* and *appearance* have deceived him: 'She's but the sign and semblance of her honour'. '…And on my eyelids shall conjecture hang/To turn all beauty into thoughts of harm.' We see Claudio's full repentance when he agrees to marry a bride whom he has not seen, and who does not unmask until he has solemnly promised to marry her.

Claudio learns his lesson in the same way that Benedick does. Claudio learns to look further than what he merely sees in front of him, and Benedick learns to think more on what he hears.

Leonato

Leonato

Leonato is Hero's father, Beatrice's uncle and guardian and Governor of Messina. He is presented, at the play's opening, as kindly and hospitable, welcoming the prince's party and greeting Don John with respect, since he is 'reconciled to the prince'. He is also presented as emotional and having no reserve about demonstrating emotions: 'A kind overflow of kindness; there are no faces truer than those that are so washed'. Another quality that is hinted at is impatience. He is too busy to listen to Borachio and Verges when they have important information for him, and instructs his nephew to 'have a care, this busy time'. He also is too eager for his daughter to be married to listen to the formalities of the ceremony- 'Come, Friar Francis, be brief...'. These traits prepare us for Leonato's reaction to Hero's denunciation and his inability to be consoled. His response to the slander of his daughter may seem rather harsh, but we have been prepared for his impulsive and hasty acceptance by his consistent characterisation: it would not be in his nature to wait and listen until all sides of the story could be heard, or to disguise his grief.

Before we condemn Leonato's response too thoroughly, we must place it in the context of the time. His relationship with his daughter is a formal one, operating strictly within the accepted conventions of the time. Hero must accept his 'advice' on a choice of marriage partner, and the marriage would be looked on partly as a financial arrangement. Hero is literally his, for Claudio to 'take' with his blessing. 'Count, take of me my daughter, and with her my fortunes.' Hero's 'shaming' within such a public forum would have made her unmarriageable, and therefore dependent on her father for the rest of her life. In addition, Leonato is a well known and respected member of society: his disgrace would have been widely known.

Despite some behaviour that leaves him open to criticism by a modern audience, Leonato remains a good-natured and kindly figure. His participation in the deception of Benedick is good-humoured and 'sporting' and his forgiveness of Claudio is generous – perhaps a little too much so. In general, the play as a whole is too lighthearted in nature to allow too sinister an interpretation of Leonato's actions.

Don Pedro

Don Pedro

Don Pedro is the eagerly awaited and much revered guest of Leonato. His presence ushers in change and turmoil for the close-knit society of Messina. His early remarks to Leonato are somewhat prophetic: 'Good Signor Leonato, are you come to meet your trouble? The fashion of the world is to avoid cost, and you encounter it.' Don Pedro functions as a catalyst figure, since he undergoes little change or development, but he is the underlying – although good-natured – reason for much change and trouble. In a literal sense, the plots begin with Don Pedro's arrival: Benedick and Claudio accompany him to Messina; he invents and engineers the plan to bring Benedick and Beatrice together; he plays a key role in initiating the romance between Claudio and Hero; his forgiveness and acceptance of his rebellious brother facilitates the near destruction of that romance. At the close of the play, however, he is much the same as at the opening, whilst his friends have undergone a transition. He functions also as a 'confidante', enabling Claudio to express his real feelings for the benefit of the audience, in ways other than soliloquy. Don Pedro is not as sentimental or poetic as Claudio, but is sympathetic and capable of solemnity. Thus Claudio is able to discuss his love for Hero, or his guilt at her death, in a way that would not be possible with Benedick, or through soliloquy alone. Don Pedro is central to the action of the play, but as a facilitator rather than a participant.

But is there any more to Don Pedro than mere facilitator to the plot? Possibly. He is presented as a character who uses human nature, and other people, to amuse himself: his wooing by proxy, his plan for Beatrice and Benedick; the repartee between his friends, are all his games – private performances directed by himself. Yet we see another side of him in the tender and somewhat cryptic dialogue between him and Beatrice. He mock-seriously offers himself as her husband and we suspect that her hasty apology for his rejection may be provoked by some offence on his part: 'But, I beseech your Grace, pardon me; I was born to speak all mirth and no matter.' It is shortly after this that he announces his plan to bring Beatrice and Benedick together. When he talks to Claudio and Leonato about

Beatrice's supposed 'passion', he is the most vehemently critical, out of the three, of Benedick, and the most extravagant in his praise of Beatrice. He even says 'I would she had bestowed this dotage on me'. These are the smallest of hints and clues, however, and you will have to make up your own mind about this particular interpretation of the Prince's character. Examined in this light, though, there is a distinct poignancy about his solitary position of observer at the end of the play, and Benedick's gleeful shout of 'Prince, thou art sad. Get thee a wife, get thee a wife!'

Don John

Don John is the villain of the play. He appears to be motivated, to some extent, by jealousy. He feels constrained and patronised by Don Pedro's 'forgiveness' and jealous of Claudio's place in his affections, and of his part in his 'overthrow'. He refers to his situation as a 'mortifying mischief' and sees himself as a caged animal, denied freedom. We are presented with little other motivation. Don John's 'bastard' position, though, compared to that of the revered 'Prince', is likely to fuel his bitterness.

Bitter and disgruntled though he may be, he would be ineffective without his helpers, Borachio and Conrade. It is Borachio who brings him news of the intended marriage. It is Borachio who proposes the elaborate plan for Hero to appear unfaithful. Don John does little more than act out his assigned role – he is not the 'brains' behind the operation. He is not, then, a villain in the true tradition, just as Claudio is no tragic hero. He is, though, a destructive force, standing in opposition to his brother. Don John seeks to destroy relationships, for his own gratification; Don Pedro seeks to *construct* relationships, for his own amusement.

Margaret

Margaret is Hero's waiting-woman. She is not an especially developed or prominent character, and yet she has a key role in the action of the play. It is she whom Claudio and Don Pedro mistake for Hero at her bedroom window. The extent to which Margaret knowingly participates in the deception is never really made clear. We are told that she was involved 'against her will', and Borachio says that she 'knew not what she did when she spoke to me'. We are left to puzzle, then, at Margaret's ready acceptance of her lover's wish to have her call him 'Claudio' and to call her 'Hero', and at her reticence during the period of Hero's 'death'. This part of the plot has also been criticised for the rather sudden revelation that Margaret has an ongoing alliance with Borachio. There is no suggestion of this earlier in the play – Borachio seems to pull it conveniently out of the air.

We hear little from Margaret until the end of Act 3, when Beatrice has been transformed into a subdued, lovelorn figure. At this point, it seems as if Margaret steps in to fill her role of the witty, fast-talking, dominant female, full of innuendo. The change seems almost a self-conscious one – 'Doth not my wit become me rarely?' and Beatrice is taken aback – 'What pace is this that thy tongue keeps?' She seems to relish teasing Beatrice about Benedick, going much further than Hero allows herself to. She clearly enjoys her part in that deception.

Margaret is a character who operates mostly as a device for the Hero/Claudio plot, but is presented in a slightly more rounded way in the context of the Beatrice/Benedick plot.

The comic characters

Comic characters

These are Dogberry and Verges and the members of the Watch. Whilst other characters are depicted in a humorous and witty manner, these characters are absurd – they are open to ridicule. They are not from the same echelon of society as Leonato and co. and so are set apart by social ranking as well as by dramatic function. Some of the comedy lies in their obvious desire to be accepted on the same social footing – particularly in the case of Dogberry. This results in his ingratiating manner towards Leonato, his inaccurate, obsequious use of vocabulary and his misinterpretation of what has been said. For example, when Leonato calls him 'tedious', he decides he has been paid a compliment... 'if I were as tedious as a king, I could find it in my heart to bestow it all of your worship'. Malapropism – the misuse of vocabulary for comic effect – and misinterpretation are the central devices for comedy in Dogberry's scenes.

These characters do have an important dramatic function, however, as well as providing the obvious laughs. It is they who uncover the deceptions of Don John, despite their incompetence. This also adds a great deal of dramatic tension and irony to the action. The audience know that the chances of Dogberry dealing competently with any villain are slim. They also know that it is very much in Leonato's interest to take the time to listen to what he is saying.

So, Dogberry, Verges and The Watchmen are the characters who resolve the situation. They also delay the resolution, however, providing tension and irony. The final irony that these characters bring is that despite their complete incompetence and stupidity, they are able to discover what the other characters cannot.

Themes and images in *Much Ado About Nothing*

Deception and disguise

Deception and disguise

Like all of Shakespeare's plays, the idea of false appearance, and the discrepancy between how things appear and how they actually are, is embedded deeply within the plot and themes. The main symbol for these ideas is the 'mask'. This is used in a literal sense in the beginning and opening acts of the play: the masque ball and the masked wedding ceremony. It is used in a less literal sense in the 'offstage' scene where Margaret and Borachio 'mask' themselves as Hero and Claudio. The symbolism is then carried through in a metaphorical sense. Beatrice and Benedick wear their 'social' masks, Hero and Don John wear their masks of silence. Most of the characters, at some point, play out a role, or indulge in the creation of an illusion.

The play is structured around forms of deception. There are two plots, and most characters play a role in both. Both plots are about a deception – one intends to build a relationship; the other intends to destroy a relationship. The plots are deceptive in themselves: the dramatic Hero/Claudio plot appears to be the central one, and yet the humorous Beatrice/Benedick plot gains most of our attention.

Each plot uses a different form of deception. Just as Claudio falls in love through his eyes, so he is deceived through his eyes. His deceptions are visual. He thinks he sees Hero with another man; he thinks he is seeing Hero's cousin as his bride. Perhaps it is significant that the one time he is deceived through his *ears* is when Don John has pretended to mistake him for Benedick. 'Thus answer I in the name of Benedick,/But hear these ill news in the name of Claudio.' Benedick himself is deceived through his ears. There are no physical disguises, just overheard conversations.

Deception is not limited to plot and characters, but is also present within Shakespeare's use of language. A study of Elizabethan word play would be too detailed to explore in full, but a look at the deceptive nature of the title can be used as an example. 'Much ado' meant much fuss or bother, and is applicable to all parts of the plot. 'Nothing', however, had several connotations. 'Nothing' and 'noting' were pronounced the same way. Therefore the play title has a double meaning – much ado about something which doesn't exist, or much ado about noticing and being perceptive – or not, in Claudio's case. You will notice that there are many references to 'noting' throughout the script, including the seemingly irrelevant wordplay on 'noting' between Balthasar and Don Pedro in Act 2, scene 3. It has also been said that the title carries sexual connotations: 'thing' was Elizabethan slang for male genitals, and therefore 'nothing' indicates the lack of them. This would fit in with the Hero/Claudio plot and Hero's insistence that she is a maid (or virgin). The play abounds with similar ambiguities of language, showing that surface appearance can be deceptive – just like the plot of the play.

All the main characters in *Much Ado About Nothing* participate in deception of some kind during the course of the play. Even Dogberry and Verges indulge in what is basically a 'play-acting' version of a courtroom trial. Disguise and deception operate on many different levels, both in a literal and a symbolic sense. They are so key that almost every other aspect of the play requires some consideration of this central theme.

Self-deception

Self-deception

Much Ado About Nothing is as much about the way people can deceive themselves as about the way they deceive others. The main self-deceivers in the play are Beatrice and Benedick. They cover their true selves with witty words and jests, declaring in sweeping terms that *nothing* would induce them to accept the love of a member of the opposite sex – particularly each other's! You may consider their 'merry war' to be simply a mask for their mutual attraction, a way of ensuring the attention of the other. There is irony in their lack of self-knowledge. They pride themselves on their quickness of wit, and yet they are easy targets for duping. Both are shocked when they hear their faults pointed out, as if they have suddenly come face to face with themselves. Their masks have been ripped away, so they can see themselves as other people do.

The other self-deceivers are Dogberry and Verges. They aspire to a far more high-ranking place in society than the one to which they belong. Their desperate attempts to sound at home in that society produce comedy. They are ignorant of their own stupidity, and full of ideas about their own self-importance. They are delighted when Leonato gives them leave to examine their villains themselves, and act up to their roles with a pomposity and ceremony which makes the 'trial' a farcical one. These characters may be absurd, but we must remember that they are not the only ones to be deceived about the way things are.

Fashion

Fashion

There is a preoccupation throughout the play with the idea of constancy, or lack of it, in friendship, love and life. The recurring motif for this theme is fashion and clothing: Conrade and Borachio discuss fashion just after Borachio's trick to make Hero appear inconstant in love; Margaret and Hero discuss the fashion of Hero's wedding gown just before her accusation of inconstancy; Don Pedro criticises Benedick's new 'fashion' just as he has changed his attitude towards love. The masque ball would have been the height of fashion of the time and is the setting for several deceptive appearances – Beatrice, Benedick, Don John, Don Pedro. The 'masks' that the characters wear for the ball are symbolic of their deceptive appearances throughout the play.

Fashion represents the outside appearance of things and its tendency to change or deceive. Fashion itself is fickle, inconstant, and liable to change on a whim, or from outside pressure – as are some of the characters in *Much Ado About Nothing*. Claudio accuses Hero of inconstancy, when in fact it is he who is inconstant in his trust and love. Beatrice accuses Benedick of inconstancy – '…he wears his faith but as the fashion of his hat' and yet Benedick turns out to be a true friend and loyal lover. Benedick, like Beatrice, is guilty only of being fickle in his views and opinions. It is this which prompts Don Pedro's scathing remarks about

Benedick's new 'fashion' as a lover: '...as to be a Dutchman today, a Frenchman tomorrow, or in the shape of two countries at once, as a German from the waist downward, all slops, and a Spaniard from the hip upward, no doublet'. It seems that, at first, Benedick takes very seriously the established 'fashion' of a courtier in love.

The references to 'fashion' and clothing in the play are a reminder of the deceptive nature of appearances, and of the way those appearances can alter to disguise the truth, or to uncover it.

Love and courtship

Love and courtship

The play explores the nature of love and compares two different types of courtship. Hero and Claudio fall in love for what they see. Their love appears to be based on physical attraction – particularly on Claudio's side. Theirs is a formal and public courtship. Leonato has to be consulted, Hero is wooed by proxy; their first real encounter is in public, surrounded by friends and family. In keeping with the formal, public nature of their engagement, Claudio decides to expose Hero's 'infidelity' on a formal and public occasion – their wedding. The emphasis is on Leonato 'giving' and Claudio 'taking' – a transaction which involves Leonato's money. Hero seems quite happy to go along with the system, even though her father has previously told her that the prince may propose. Real understanding and compatibility is not an issue at this stage: this is left till later. The main thing is to get Hero married off to someone of worth and standing, and Claudio fits the bill as well as the prince did.

Beatrice and Benedick are not obliged to conduct their courtship within society's rules. Money is not a part of their marital arrangement, since Beatrice is not Leonato's heir, and Benedick's finances are not mentioned. Benedick consults with Leonato, but Leonato is clearly less worried about Beatrice's 'match'. Hero happily accepts what she is presented with, while Beatrice is more demanding: she expects absolute loyalty from her lover and her command of 'kill Claudio' is a test to see if Benedick is up to the job. Despite being 'tricked' into their love, it is not one based merely on physical attraction: they have known each other as old enemies. Benedick is able to appreciate Beatrice's beauty whilst acknowledging that it is not enough. '...were she not possessed with a fury, exceeds her (Hero) as much in beauty as the first of May doth the last of December'. Beatrice and Benedick fall in love with their ears rather than their eyes, for it is what is what they hear, in praise of each other, which helps them to recognise their worth.

Hero and Claudio *appear* to choose to marry each other, but they are really just playing by society's rules. Beatrice and Benedick appear to be tricked into their romance and yet, perhaps, they are the ones who are exercising their personal freedom and choice. The irony, once more, lies in the discrepancy between appearance and reality.

■ Text commentary

Act 1, scene 1

The play opens in Messina and the action remains here throughout. The choice of location, however, is somewhat nominal. The Italianate setting perhaps adds a touch of romance and escapism to the play, but it is less important to the plot than some of Shakespeare's other dramas.

Leonato, governor of Messina, is accompanied by his daughter and niece when he receives news that Don Pedro, Prince of Arragon, is to arrive that night, following a recent military victory. We learn that Don Pedro has cultivated a friendship with one of his best soldiers, a young Florentine named Claudio, who also has connections in Messina. Leonato's niece, Beatrice, asks scathingly after Benedick of Padua, and it transpires that he too is a good friend of Claudio's.

The military party arrives. It consists of Don Pedro, Claudio, Benedick and Don John, Don Pedro's illegitimate half-brother, who has just been 'reconciled' to his brother after the recent war. Hero, Leonato's daughter, is introduced to the party and Beatrice initiates a witty and insulting argument with Benedick.

Benedick and Claudio are left alone and Claudio reveals his desire for Hero. Benedick is not impressed, and expresses his revulsion for the idea of marriage. Don Pedro arrives and is informed of Claudio's love for Hero. He approves, and when Benedick departs, Claudio is able to discuss the depth of his love to a sympathetic listener. Don Pedro offers to disguise himself as Claudio at that night's party and woo Hero for him.

'I pray you, is Signor Montanto returned from the wars or no?'

This is Beatrice's opening line and it is typical of her quick, forthright speech which is riddled with puns and innuendo. 'Montanto' is a fencing term, and by referring to Benedick in this way she is mocking his fighting ability. Her dismissive 'or no?' implies a nonchalance about Benedick's return – and indeed, about whether he is dead or alive. You should note, though, that Beatrice asks the question, unprompted, as soon as she has the opportunity. What might this suggest to you about her interest in Benedick? She goes on to inform the astonished messenger that Benedick is a fickle character who changes allegiance easily. The messenger's response, though, shows that he has heard nothing but good of Benedick. When the party arrives, Beatrice addresses Benedick first, again uninvited, in the form of a

Benedick

devastating insult. Beatrice and Benedick's first comments to each other imply an ongoing feud, and the audience has already been prepared for their 'merry war' by Leonato. There is also some ironic foreshadowing of events in Leonato's comment that Beatrice will never 'run mad' (succumb to the 'pestilence' of Benedick).

Consider Beatrice's motivations in enquiring after Benedick, and relentlessly criticising him – especially his fidelity in friendship. In some ways, the Beatrice/Benedick plot is a comedy of human nature. Their relationship could be easily transposed onto a modern day situation: this universal nature is part of the appeal of the comedy.

The play's central devices/themes of deception are introduced here. A

Self-deception

subtle form of dramatic irony is at work in the discrepancy between what we, the audience, may feel we know about Beatrice's motivations and feelings, and what Beatrice does. This, of course, will depend on the direction of the performance: a director may choose to play down the history of their attraction for each other, but there is certainly scope for some sparks of sexual chemistry to emerge!

'…there's her cousin, an' she were not possessed with a fury, exceeds her as much in beauty as the first of May doth the last of December.'

So far we have seen how Beatrice's sudden passion for Benedick is hinted at right from the beginning. In the quotation above, we can also see how Shakespeare provides the seeds for Benedick's love to grow. He dismisses Claudio's love for Hero, unable to see the attraction, but acknowledges Beatrice's beauty. These clues, provided early in the play, make the ensuing Benedick/Beatrice match credible as well as hilarious.

'I will see you, 'ere I die, look pale with love.'

Benedick follows his statement about Beatrice with an outright rejection of

Benedick

love and marriage, to the amusement of Don Pedro, who is prompted to set himself the challenge of seeing Benedick 'look pale with love.' The exchange between the three is amusing, and as well as setting up expectations for the audience in terms of plot, marks Benedick out as defiantly 'one of the lads', disappointed that his friend has succumbed to the temptations of matrimony. His astonishment and disappointment is comic and again, easy to imagine in a modern-day context. Do you feel that Benedick is a more likeable character than the lovesick Claudio, though? The differences in their speech parallel the differences in their outlooks. Claudio often speaks in delicately phrased blank verse, which contrasts with Benedick's sharp-tongued prose.

'Hath Leonato any son, my lord?'

Claudio's question about whether Hero will inherit her father's money may

Love and
courtship

lead you to question his motives. It should be remembered, though, that it was acceptable for marriage to be considered a financial arrangement between two families, and open discussion of this would not be unusual. It is worth bearing this in mind, however, when subsequent events concerning Claudio and Hero come to light. Add to this Claudio's next speech, in blank verse. He tells Don Pedro that he has not pursued Hero before because he had military plans to take care of, but now they are finished, he can turn his thoughts to love. It is not clear, though, to whom Claudio is trying to justify his actions – or lack of them. To Don Pedro? Or to himself? Or, possibly, this is a way of giving his love credibility to us, the audience.

'I will assume thy part in some disguise'

The first part in the Hero/Claudio plot is revealed here and explained to us

Don Pedro

Deception and
disguise

by Don Pedro. It is notable that Don Pedro has introduced us to both of the parallel plots: he has challenged himself to see Benedick 'look pale with love', and he has offered to mediate between Claudio and Hero. In this way he is a catalyst to both plots. To a modern–day audience Don Pedro's offer may see strange and lacking in credibility. You will need to take several factors into account, however. First of all, the party is to be a 'masque' where everyone assumes some disguise anyway. Secondly, Claudio has clearly spent much of his time fulfilling a purely military function, not allowing himself to turn his thoughts to love – so he is an inexperienced lover and may not be as successful in his wooing as the more worldly Don Pedro. Added to this is the fact that wooing by 'proxy' was not such a bizarre idea in Shakespeare's day as it may seem today!

'My cousin means Signor Benedick of Padua.'

A strikingly odd parallel can be drawn between the two characters of Don

Hero

John and Hero. Both remain mostly silent in this scene, apart from one line. Arguably, both their silences are devices for concealment. Hero's silence is that of submission. She stands quietly through the discussion of her parentage, and the reader is left to guess what her expression would be whilst the banter takes place. This highlights the contrast between Hero and her more aggressive cousin. Whilst Beatrice covers her feelings and identity with a multitude of words and jests, Hero covers her own identity (which emerges more clearly later on) with silence.

'…I am not of many words, but I thank you.'

Don John

Don John, too, conceals his true feelings and intentions behind a *lack* of words, but his silence is a sinister and brooding one. At the end of this scene, Don John and Hero are left relatively unveiled for the audience. Neither has been extensively revealed by other characters, and they give little away themselves. Hero's silence has become the subject of debate between critics of the play. You will need to decide for yourself whether it is the silence of a strong, but reticent, character, or the silence of a weak and malleable one.

'… he wears his faith but as the fashion of his hat; it ever changes with the next block.'

The scene introduces us to one of the play's main concerns – constancy and inconstancy in love, friendship and to oneself. Beatrice criticises Benedick for being fickle. Later, Claudio, punning on Benedick's joke about Hero being short, hopes that he will stay faithful in his desire for Hero. We find later that Claudio is not always as constant and loyal in his love as he believes himself, but that Benedick is inconstant only to himself.

Fashion

The motif of 'fashion' is often used to highlight this theme. Fashion is inconstant and changes to suit society and general opinion. The 'masque' was the height of fashion and the use of this as a springboard for the plot suitably underlines the idea of outward appearances being deceptive. There are two direct references to fashion in this first scene: Beatrice's comment on Benedick, and Don Pedro's comment to Leonato that it is the 'fashion of the world to avoid cost and you encounter it', perhaps foreshadowing later troublesome events which are, indeed, caused by Don Pedro's party.

Act 1, scene 2

Leonato meets his brother, Antonio. One of Antonio's employees has overheard the conversation between Claudio and Leonato and reported back to him. Antonio passes the information on to his brother, but tells him that it is Don Pedro who seeks to woo Hero. Leonato treats the information with caution, but says that he will forewarn his daughter.

'But brother, I can tell you strange news that you yet dreamt not of.'

This is the first example of false report in the play – albeit an accidental one.

Its purpose is not entirely clear – why would Hero need to be prepared to answer Don Pedro, and not Claudio? It is perhaps included purely to begin to build on the atmosphere of confusion and miscommunication and to highlight the themes of deception and disguise. Alternatively, it could be to show the fickle nature of love: Hero is prepared to accept Don Pedro, but just as happily settles for Claudio.

'...but they have a good cover; they show well outward.'

Antonio's comment on the news he is about to impart further underlines the central theme of deception, and the discrepancy between appearance and reality. The events are to be unveiled at the masque that night. This is significant, because the masque is representative of just how deceptive outward appearances can be.

Deception and disguise

Act 1, scene 3

Don John and his companion Conrade enter. Conrade asks Don John why he seems so uneasy and he replies that he is not happy with his subordinate position in life and likens himself to a muzzled beast. He tells Conrade that he is not able to appear cheerful while he feels like this, or to make any show of goodwill, even to advance his own position. Borachio then enters. He, too, has overheard the conversation between Claudio and Don Pedro. He imparts the news to Don John, who welcomes it as fuel for his mischief-making against his brother and friends.

'...goest about to apply a moral medicine to a mortifying mischief.'

Don John begins to reveal his character to us through this dialogue with

Borachio. Don John is a relatively undeveloped character in the play, but he is provided with motivation for his wrongdoings. When he refers to the 'mortifying mischief' and when he talks about the 'occasion that breeds', he is referring to his subordinate position in life: he is Don Pedro's illegitimate half-brother, and therefore not accepted by society; he has been beaten in an attempt to overpower his brother; he is now reliant on Don Pedro's goodwill. His jealousy of Don Pedro and Claudio and his desire for revenge motivate his actions. Do you find these are credible reasons? Or do you think they are frail justifications for a wholly evil character?

Don John

'I cannot hide what I am'

There is some irony in this comment. Don John describes himself as a 'plain-dealing villain' and in some ways he is right: by being of 'few words', he does not try to ingratiate himself with Don Pedro's friends, or pretend that he is happy with his situation. The irony lies in his function as arch deceiver of the play. It is he who performs the main deception in the Hero/Claudio plot by feigning concern over Claudio's future happiness.

Deception and disguise

'...It is needful that you frame the season for your own harvest.' *Conrade*
'I had rather be a canker in a hedge than a rose in his grace.' *Don John*

Both characters use images of nature to illustrate their speech. This has the effect of giving the dialogue an uneasy, sinister feel. There is something distorted in Conrade's image of a 'harvest' for Don John's evil plans and something unsettling about Don John's juxtapositioning of 'rose' and 'canker' (plant disease). Nature imagery is often associated with freedom, growth and renewal, but its association here with the evil plans of the pair seems to distort this meaning and highlights the bitter, warped nature of the two men.

'...that young start-up hath all the glory of my overthrow.'
'Let us to the great supper: their cheer is the greater that I am subdued. Would the cook were of my mind!'

These two comments by Don John clearly reveal his bitterness and jealousy of Claudio. By the end of the scene, the audience expects Don John to make trouble. In this way, Shakespeare has created tension very early on. There is also a certain amount of dramatic irony which feeds into this. The audience has been privy to this exchange, but it has been concealed from the other characters, who expect nothing.

Don John

Don John exits with a devastatingly bitter comment: he complains that the others take delight in his downfall, and wishes the cook felt as he does so that he could poison them!

Consider again Don John's motives and nature. Do you feel any sympathy for him? Or do you think Shakespeare wanted us to see him as a simple 'villain'?

Self-test Questions Act One

Uncover the plot
Delete two of the three alternatives given to find the correct plot. Beware possible misconceptions and muddles.
Leonato, Prince/King/Governor of Messina, learns of the arrival of Don Pedro/

Claudio/Don John, who is Prince of Messina/Florence/Arragon. He is to arrive with his friend Claudio/Borachio/Don John. When he arrives he also brings his brother/cousin/uncle Don John and another soldier, Benedick/Balthasar/Conrade.

Leonato is accompanied by his daughter/cousin/wife Hero and her sister/friend/cousin Beatrice. Beatrice argues with Benedick/Balthasar/Conrade and we find out that Beatrice has always been friends with/taken an instant dislike to/had a long-running feud with him. Leonato welcomes all the visitors, but gives a special welcome to Don John, who is of a talkative/reserved/noisy nature. Claudio/Borachio/Don John confesses to Benedick/Balthasar/Conrade that he loves Hero. Benedick/Balthasar/Conrade encourages the romance/is disappointed with his friend/is not interested and says that he, himself, wishes to marry/will never marry/intends to become a monk. He also says that Beatrice is more attractive than/uglier than/taller than Hero. Don Pedro is sympathetic to Claudio/Borachio/Don John and tells him that he will lend them money/arrange an elopement for them/woo Hero on his behalf.

Leonato meets his brother/father/cousin, Antonio, who tells him that he has heard that Claudio/Don Pedro/Benedick wishes to marry Hero. Don John speaks in private to Conrade and tells him that he wishes to make mischief/make trouble for his brother/make amends. The plan for the marriage was also overheard by Leonato/Borachio/Conrade, and Don John resolves to kill him/congratulate him/use the information to hurt him.

Who? What? Why? When? Where? How?

1 Who has '…borne himself beyond the promise of his age'?
2 Why does the messenger wish to 'hold friends' with Beatrice?
3 How does Beatrice refer to Benedick when she first asks after him?
4 Who is 'not of many words'?
5 What does Don Pedro volunteer to do for Claudio?
6 Why does Claudio ask Don Pedro if Leonato has a son?
7 Where were Don Pedro and Claudio overheard by Leonato's servant?
8 Who else overheard the conversation between Claudio and Don Pedro?
9 Why is Don John so displeased with Claudio?
10 What planet does Don John claim he was born under, and what significance has this?

Who said that?

1 'How much better is it to weep at joy than to joy at weeping?'
2 'I pray you, is Signor Montanto returned from the wars or no?'
3 '… the fashion of the world is to avoid cost and you encounter it.'
4 'I had rather hear my dog bark at a crow than hear a man swear he loves me.'
5 'In mine eye, she is the sweetest lady I ever looked on.'
6 'Shall I never see a bachelor of threescore again?'
7 'In time, the savage bull doth bear the yoke.'
8 'There is no measure in the occasion that breeds it; therefore the sadness is without limit.'
9 'That young start-up hath all the glory of my overthrow.'

Open quotes

Identify the scene; complete the phrase; identify the speaker and the character being spoken to.

1 'I pray you, how many hath he killed and eaten in these wars…'
2 'And a good soldier to a lady. But…'
3 'He is most in the company of…'
4 'If he have caught Benedick…'

5   'You always end with a jade's trick...'
6   'I dare swear he is no hypocrite....'
7   'As the event stamps them...'(complete sentence)
8   'I must be sad when I have cause and smile at no man's jests...'
9   'If I had my mouth, I would bite; If I had my liberty...'
10 'To the death...'

Act 2, scene 1

This is a long and complex scene which draws together the different aspects of the plots, and paves the way for new developments.

Just before the dance begins, Leonato, Antonio and Beatrice discuss the relative merits of Benedick and Don John, concluding that a mixture of the only good qualities of both might make the perfect man. Beatrice then announces her gratitude for her unmarried state and Hero is prevailed upon by both Antonio and Leonato to accept the prince if he should ask her to marry him.

The masque begins, and the four are joined by several other characters. All are wearing masks. There follows a series of exchanges which have mistaken identity as a common link: firstly, Antonio tries to withhold his identity from Margaret; next, Beatrice and Benedick hold an insulting conversation under the pretence of not recognising one another; lastly, Don John approaches Claudio, pretending to think that he is Benedick, and tells him that Don Pedro is wooing Hero for himself. Claudio is hurt and outraged, but much relieved later when he discovers that the information is false. The date of the marriage is set, with Leonato's blessing, for the following Monday.

Towards the end of the scene, Don Pedro announces that he will make the time until Claudio's wedding go more quickly by playing the part of matchmaker between Benedick and Beatrice. He enlists the help of his friends and so one of the two major deceptions of the play begins to unfold.

'The revellers are entering, brother; make good room.'

The masque is central to the play and although it is by no means the climax,

Deception and disguise

it gathers together all the strands of Act 1 and provides a springboard for the events to follow: Don John's attempt to destroy the marriage has failed, but the audience knows of his evil intentions – unlike the ignorant Hero and Claudio; Don Pedro has officially announced his plan of bringing Beatrice and Benedick together. Thus the two distinct plots evolve.

You should note here the opposition within the structure of the play. One plan aims to bring about a marriage; one intends to destroy a marriage.

There is often some debate around the issue of which is the main plot of the play. Do you think, at this stage, they seem to have equal status, or is one more of a 'sub-plot' than the other? It is often said that the Hero/Claudio plot forms the substance of the drama and should be considered to be the main plot, and yet the Beatrice/Benedick plot often seems more appealing. Which one intrigues you most, and why? Continue to ask yourself this as you read on.

'Thus answer I in the name of Benedick, But hear these ill news with the ears of Claudio.' (Hero/Claudio plot) 'The Prince's fool? Ha!...' (Beatrice/Benedick plot)

Even though the plots are in opposition to each other, they are both built on false identity and confusion. The lighthearted atmosphere of mayhem which the masque produces is a good background for this and is symbolic of the central idea of disguise and deception. This levity of atmosphere can be sustained even when the more sinister deception has taken place. For example, Claudio's outrage at his 'betrayal' is diluted by Benedick's sharp and slightly mocking comments, and his own comic indignation at Beatrice's insults. This is open to interpretation, though, and so you should consider how you would direct this part. Would you play up the comedy? Or would you try to convey the seriousness of the situation? How? Would you want Claudio played as an easily led fool, or would you make his situation seem credible, and therefore build sympathy for him? Again, how would you do this?

'He were an excellent man that were made just in the midway between him and Benedick...'

There is another opportunity here for you to examine Beatrice's feelings and

Beatrice

motives. Leonato and Antonio were discussing Don John, not Benedick, and yet Beatrice brings his name into the conversation, just as she did in Act 1. Do you feel, perhaps, that you know more about Beatrice's feelings than Beatrice herself does? The 'deception' element of the play includes deception of the self, as well as deception of others. Do you think you can find the same signs of self-deception in Benedick? Have a look at Benedick's reaction to Beatrice's comments, and the way in which he seems unable to be sympathetic to his friend while he is thinking of this (lines 181-192).

'Just if he sends me no husband; for the which blessing I am at my knees every morning and evening.'

Beatrice's sweeping statement matches Benedick's in Act 1, when he declares that if he ever marries, then he should be given horns, painted 'vilely' and

Love and
courtship

generally ridiculed in public (lines 242-248). Look also at Benedick's long speech between lines 219 and 239, where he announces outright that he would not marry Beatrice if she had all the temptations of Eve. The brashness of their opinions and their overt dislike of each other gives the outcome of the play its comic irony, as well as teaching both of them a lesson!

'Indeed, my Lord, he lent it me awhile, and I gave him use for it, a double heart for his single one. Marry, once before he won it of me with false dice'

What do you make of this speech by Beatrice? Is she indicating here that she and Benedick had previously been lovers, or had a minor flirtation? How do you think Benedick would have won her heart with 'false dice'? There appear to be no correct answers to these questions – the audience is left to puzzle over their history. Try filling in the gaps yourself.

'No, sure, my lord, my mother cried; but then there was a star danced, and under that was I born.'

Around this point we seem to see a different side to Beatrice. Through this

Beatrice

beautifully balanced sentence we have a glimpse of a more vulnerable side of her nature. Compare this with Leonato's comment that she 'often dreamt of unhappiness and waked herself with laughing'. Examine her concern for Claudio and her quickness to clear up misunderstanding with a witty pun: '...civil as an orange, and something of that jealous complexion'. Lastly, think about what qualities Don Pedro must have seen in her in order to offer himself as her husband – possibly in earnest. Do you feel that you have a more rounded picture of Beatrice now than you did earlier in the scene?

Act 2, scene 2

Don John and Borachio discuss the failure of their plans to wreck Claudio's marriage. Borachio claims he has a second plan to hand and that this time he cannot fail. He tells Don John that he has won the confidence of Margaret, Hero's waiting-woman. He says that he will arrange for them both to appear at Hero's chamber window at an appointed time. Meanwhile, Don John should arrange for the prince and Claudio to wait with him outside the house. He claims that it will be easy to mistake Margaret for Hero, and so make it appear that Hero has been unfaithful. Don John approves the plan, and offers Borachio a thousand ducats if it should prove successful.

'I am sick in displeasure to him, and whatsoever comes athwart his affection ranges evenly with mine.'

Don John

The atmosphere again switches abruptly from the lighthearted merriment of the previous scene to the sinister feel of Don John's scheming. Don John, here, freely expresses his revulsion for Claudio, and you may feel that the motivating factor of jealousy is becoming clearer.

'...hear me call Margaret Hero, hear Margaret term me Claudio.'

The two ideas of disguise and deception are drawn together here to produce

Deception and disguise

the 'destructive' side of the play. Don John intends to deceive Benedick and Claudio by claiming genuinely to believe in her infidelity, and Borachio intends to 'disguise' Margaret as Hero. The extent of Margaret's own knowledge of this plan is never really made clear. Later on in the play, Leonato comments on her participation being 'against her will'. Does this mean that she was coerced, or that she had no knowledge of the plan? As you read on, you will need to decide for yourself.

Margaret

Margaret is not an especially well-drawn character, but she plays a crucial role in the initiation of both main deceptions. Her role as waiting-woman is an important one, as it gives her an access to the two main female characters that the others would not have. In this way she is more a device than a character in her own right.

Act 2, scene 3

Benedick is walking in the orchard, contemplating Claudio's fickle nature. He laments that his friend could be so easily lured by romance when he has already laughed at others in love. Benedick declares that he will never be caught out like this himself.

Don Pedro, Leonato and Claudio approach, and Benedick, unable to face the lovesick Claudio, hides in an arbour. The three are aware of his presence, however, and, after persuading Balthasar to sing, begin to talk of Beatrice's supposed 'love' for Benedick. Benedick is shocked, but the trick works and he declares abruptly that he will return her love. Don Pedro, Claudio and Leonato disappear and Beatrice comes to call Benedick in for dinner. Benedick's attitude towards Beatrice in this interaction is transformed into a meek and polite one.

'...and such a man is Claudio.'

This is part of Benedick's hugely ironic speech which builds up to the transformation to come. We have already heard him talk contemptuously of

Benedick

love and lovers; now he reinforces those views with a long soliloquy in prose which rails against the hypocrisy of Claudio for turning from soldier to lover. Benedick flatly announces that nothing short of a goddess would make him turn in the same way. The comic tension is heightened here by the audience's foreknowledge that the deception is about to take place, and their suspicion of the very likely outcome of it.

'Men were deceivers ever.'

Balthasar's song is significant in its theme of deception and inconstancy

Self-deception

amongst men. Benedick is about to be tricked into an inconstancy of his own nature, and Claudio is also to be tricked into inconstancy against Hero. Look also at the play on the words 'note', 'nothing' and 'noting' when Balthasar is persuaded to sing. 'Noting' and 'nothing' were pronounced the same way, and thus could be interchangeable in meaning. This links with the title of the play, which also could be taken to have either meaning.

'I should think this a gull, but that the white-bearded fellow speaks it; knavery cannot, sure, hide itself in such reverence.'

Benedick is completely fooled by the trickery. His acceptance of what the

Leonato

others say is given more credibility, both to him and to the audience, by the involvement of Leonato, a respected figure who would not normally participate in such frivolity. Perhaps this 'extra' touch is necessary in order to preserve our perception of Benedick as a sharp-witted character, even though in this instance he is being ridiculed.

'He doth, indeed, show some sparks that are like wit.'

It is interesting to note the tenor of Don Pedro's remarks at this point. He

Don Pedro

seems to undermine Benedick a great deal, whilst his other friends are much kinder towards him. Look also at his comment 'I would she had bestowed this dotage on me'. Do you think his comments might have something to do with his previous offer of marriage to Beatrice? Is there a bitter tone to them, or is he merely teasing his friend? What do you think might be his thoughts and feelings at this time?

'Love me? Why, it must be requited.'

Benedick now embarks on his second long soliloquy of the scene, in direct contrast to the first. He is completely fooled, and determines to return Beatrice's love. This completes the irony of the scene: Benedick has followed

Benedick

Claudio in his transformation from soldier to lover, just minutes after condemning his friend's behaviour. He had announced previously that he would not marry unless he found a woman who was fair, wise and virtuous, and now he convinces himself that he has found all three in Beatrice – despite what he said about her in the past. Again, Shakespeare tries to prevent Benedick from being perceived as a total fool by having him acknowledge his turnabout, and the criticisms he may face. He begins a process of justification in his own head. 'When I said I would die a bachelor, I did not think I would live till I were married,' he states. In addition to the comic effect this produces, it also stops us from regarding Benedick as a simpleton. He acknowledges his weakness, but the desire to love and be loved has won over his stubbornness.

What do you make of Benedick's conversion? Is it what you have been prepared for? Or do you think it is too sudden and unrealistic to be credible? The situation may lack credibility, but the sentiment and the circumstance are ones with which many people may identify.

Self-test Questions Act Two

Uncover the plot
Delete two of the three alternatives given, to find the correct plot. Beware possible misconceptions and muddles.

Leonato's family prepare for their party. Leonato reminds Hero that if Claudio/Don Pedro/Othello should ask her to marry him, she should say perhaps/yes/no. At the party Don Pedro takes Hero aside and woos her for Macbeth/Benedick/Claudio. Unfortunately, because of Don John's/Borachio's/Leonata's interference, Claudio believes that Don Pedro has hypnotised her/wooed Hero for himself/run away with her. Beatrice meets Benedick in disguise and the two exchange money/compliments/insults. After Don Pedro has assured Claudio that he has not tricked him, he and Hero/Beatrice/Ophelia arrange to marry on Monday/next month/at Christmas. Claudio wants to marry that night/the next day/the next year, because he feels that a week/month/year is too long to wait. Don Pedro announces that he will try to make a match between Benedick and Rosalind/Beatrice/himself.

Conrade/Borachio/Banquo has a plan to help Don John destroy Claudio's marriage. He will ask Margaret, Hero's waiting-woman/sister/daughter, to appear with him at Hero's door/at her chamber window/in her garden the next day/the next night/the night before the wedding. It will then seem as if Hero has been unfaithful to Claudio/will prove her faithfulness/make a fool of Hero.

When Benedick sees Claudio and his friends approaching, he hides in a hole/shed/arbour. His friends laugh at him/pretend not to see him/greet him and start talking loudly about Beatrice's love for him/Claudio's marriage/the weather. Benedick is bored/shocked/not surprised, but convinces himself that he must run away/tell her he is not interested/love her back.

Who? What? Why? When? Where? How?
1 Who does Beatrice think would make an 'excellent man'?
2 Why does Don Pedro pair off with Hero?
3 Who does Antonio talk to at the Masque?
4 Who is the 'prince's fool'?
5 Who does Don John pretend to think Claudio is?
6 Why does he do this?
7 How long does Claudio have to wait to marry Hero?
8 How much does Don John pay Borachio for carrying out his plan?
9 Who try to trick Benedick into falling in love with Beatrice? (three people)
10 What is it that makes Benedick believe he is not being tricked?

Who said that?
1 'Speak low, if you speak love.'
2 'God match me with a good dancer!'
3 'Well, I'll be revenged as I may.'
4 'The transgression is in the stealer.'
5 'If her breath were as terrible as her terminations, there were no living near her'
6 '…you have lost the heart of Signor Benedick.'
7 '…my cunning shall not shame me.'
8 'How canst thou cross this marriage?'
9 'A man loves the meat in his youth that he cannot endure in his old age.'
10 '…there's a double meaning in that!'

Open quotes
Identify the scene; complete the phrase; identify the speaker and the character being spoken to.
1 'How tartly that gentleman looks! I can never see him but…'
2 '…let him be a handsome fellow, or else make another…'
3 'If the Prince do solicit you in that kind…'
4 'Thus answer I in the name of Benedick…'(next line)
5 'O, she misused me past the endurance of…'
6 'I cannot endure my…'
7 'Indeed, my lord, he lent it me awhile…'
8 '…she hath often dreamt of unhappiness…'
9 'Proof enough to misuse the Prince…'
10 'I will, in the interim, undertake one of Hercules' labours…'

Act 3, scene 1

The parallel deception now takes place. Hero asks her waiting-woman, Margaret, to find Beatrice and tell her that she is being discussed by Hero and Ursula. She correctly guesses that Beatrice will be unable to resist wanting to hear what is being said about her. Hero then instructs Ursula to talk about Benedick's virtues, making sure that Beatrice can hear, and making clear that she hears of Benedick's love for her.

They carry out their plan, adding that Beatrice is too proud and unkind to be deserved by such a man. Beatrice, like Benedick, is overwhelmed. She unquestioningly accepts what she has heard and resolves to return Benedick's love fully.

**'Then go we near her, that her ear lose nothing
Of the false sweet bait that we lay for it.'**

We see a whole new side to Hero now. She has previously had very little to say. Her speeches have been little more than a couple of lines each, usually in direct response to a question. Suddenly, however, she is issuing instructions, using poetic language and declaring her opinions. Are there any reasons for this change? Notice that in this scene Hero converses only with other women. Do you think this might make a difference to her behaviour? Or is it truly that her love and goodwill for Beatrice have given her boldness and enthusiasm? Is this the real Hero, or is she merely playing another role? See below for another possible clue.

Hero

'Disdain and scorn ride sparkling in her eyes...'

Hero comes up with some pretty scathing comments about Beatrice at this point. She has said that her desire is to help her cousin find a husband, but now she seems to want to point out all Beatrice's faults – something she would never dare do under ordinary circumstances. There is no doubt of Hero's real affection for Beatrice, but she seems to gather momentum when she points out her cousin's shortcomings. Beatrice '...cannot love...', is 'self-endeared' and thinks herself so smart that '...all else seems weak'. Hero then adds that if she were to tell Beatrice this, she would be scorned and mocked by her. She says this, of course, knowing full well that she really *is* telling Beatrice all these things about herself and that Beatrice cannot very well do anything about it!

Do you think Hero goes a little over the top here? Is it necessary to be quite so hard on Beatrice, in order to match her up with Benedick? Why might Hero feel the need to say these things? You could compare Hero's speeches with Don Pedro's complaints about Benedick in the previous scene. Both are loyal friends, but might possibly have cause to feel frustrated with their respective companions.

**'...Of this matter
Is little Cupid's crafty arrow made,
That only wounds by hearsay.'**

This is one of several occurrences of deception by false report in the play. The situations are potentially ridiculous, and yet the audience is able to believe in them. The whole situation here seems plausible to us because of Shakespeare's clever understanding of human nature. We all know how hard it is to resist listening to a conversation about ourselves – and this would especially apply to a proud, impetuous character like Beatrice. We may

Beatrice

also have found that other people's opinions influence our own – and so Hero's praise of Benedick is liable to raise him in Beatrice's esteem. Do you find yourself able to identify with Beatrice here?

'And, Benedick, love on...'

Was Hero's 'trick' really all it took for Beatrice to fall for Benedick? Remind

yourself of the clues you found earlier which suggested that the seeds may have already been sown in Beatrice's own mind. One idea is that it is only Beatrice's pride that has been tricked by Hero – she has just been made to admit to her affection. The easy duping of both Benedick and Beatrice shows, at the

Self-deception very least, how closely hate is linked to love. The 'appearance' of the couple's hatred for each other has easily been transformed into love.

Act 3, scene 2

This scene takes place on the eve of Claudio's wedding to Hero. Benedick's friends gather to tease Benedick about his transformed state. They, of course, know very well why he has become so serious, but continue to conjecture, guess and tease as if they didn't. Benedick claims he has toothache and then draws Leonato aside to speak to him privately. Don Pedro suspects that Benedick wants to talk to him about marrying Beatrice.

Don John enters. He tells Claudio that Hero has been unfaithful, and that if he wants to see evidence of this he should join Don John that night, outside her chamber window. Claudio agrees, and Don Pedro says that he will support him.

'Gallants, I am not as I have been.'

Benedick is indeed a changed man. Compare his contribution to the jests and

conversation in this scene to those before it. He contributes to the dialogue just five times, in the briefest possible manner. Turn back to Act 1 and note his levity and wordiness before his 'transformation'. He is now uttering only rather short and cryptic speeches – worthy of Don John! He has also changed

Benedick the manner of his appearance – to that which he feels befits a serious young lover. How seriously do you take this new manner? Do you feel that his rather melodramatic reaction lends the situation a comic feel?

'Disloyal?'

How do you feel about Claudio's reaction here? It takes very little to convince him of Hero's disloyalty – or, at least, of the possibility of it. It is particularly strange that both he and Don Pedro are willing to believe the man who tried to trick them at the masque. Claudio's response, in fact, is much the same as then, and his gullibility is partly what enables Don John to continue his

Claudio

wickedness. However clever a villain may be, he can do nothing without the naivete and fallibility of his victims. The character of Claudio needed to be provided with a certain amount of shallow feeling and gullibility in order to make Don John's trick plausible. Think back to Claudio's previous speeches about his feelings for Hero, and consider whether they provide enough hints for consistent characterisation.

There is also a strong irony at work here, centred around the idea of disloyalty and deceptive appearances. Hero is accused of disloyalty, and yet it is her accusers themselves who are disloyal. Don John is disloyal to his brother and his friends, and Claudio is disloyal to Hero herself, by placing hearsay before his trust for her. Hero, in fact, goes on to prove herself one of the most loyal characters in the play. She is not the only character to be accused of disloyalty in the play. Benedick has already been accused by Beatrice of disloyalty and 'fickleness' with regard to his own companions. There is an ironic twist to this, also, because although she remains steadfastly loyal to Hero, Beatrice will later demand that Benedick choose between loyalty to her and loyalty to his friends.

Act 3, scene 3

The local constable, Dogberry, and his assistant Verges enter. They brief the nightwatchmen on their duties. Since this is the night before Hero's wedding, they are issued a special duty to watch Leonato's house. Later, the watchmen overhear Borachio outlining his evil deception of Claudio to Conrade. They step forward and arrest them both.

Enter Dogberry and his partner Verges with the Watch.

This scene offers some comic relief after the heightened tension of the last

Comic characters

scene. This pattern continues throughout, with the same characters providing comedy and absurdity among the more dramatic scenes. Unlike some of Shakespeare's 'comic interlude' characters, however, this is not their only function. Dogberry and Verges are central to the plot in that they further complicate it, and delay a resolution. In some ways they are the heroes of the play: they prevent Borachio's plan from going undetected. But because of their bumbling incompetence, they allow the deception to continue much longer than it should. Their foolishness is, in fact, essential to the plot. Thus they are both 'clown' figures who make a significant contribution to the plot.

'You are thought here to be the most senseless and fit man for the constable of the watch'

Much of the humour here depends on the use of the *malapropism*, which is liberally sprinkled throughout scenes with Dogberry and Verges. This is a device where an inappropriate word is substituted for the correct one, by an apparent slip of the tongue or through a confusion of the vocabulary. Often this happens when a character is trying to appear grander or better educated than they really are. The comic irony, of course, lies in the 'mistake' word often being better suited – as above, where Dogberry is probably trying to say 'sensible'. Later on, he declares that 'for the watch to babble and talk is most tolerable and not to be endured'. We know that he actually doesn't understand the word 'tolerable', because he wants its opposite meaning. We also know that 'not to be endured' is merely a repetition of what he meant in the first place. Thus, Dogberry's attempts to be grand and articulate are rather laughable and, for the audience, produce the opposite effect of what

he intends. We have the impression of someone rather carried away by their position of authority, but who isn't quite up to the job! In this way, Dogberry continues the idea of self-deception in the play: he isn't quite what he thinks he is. As with Beatrice and Benedick, we, the audience, know better.

Self-deception   What other examples of this device can you find in this scene?

'Yes, the fashion is the fashion.'

Play close attention to Conrade and Borachio's rather rambling and frivolous

discussion of fashion – the symbol of deception and of inconstancy. It serves two purposes. First, it reminds the audience of the atmosphere of disguise, deception and illusion in which the characters operate – remember, we have been introduced to it in this context before. Secondly, it functions

Fashion   as a 'delaying' tactic, thus heightening tension. The watchmen are waiting with bated breath to hear Borachio's confession of evil – and so are the audience!

'Not so, neither: but know that I have tonight wooed Margaret, the Lady Hero's gentlewoman, by the name of Hero.'

Finally Borachio tells the story, and the watchmen are able to jump out and arrest him. Borachio's account serves as a confirmation of the plot. Notice that the whole 'wooing' episode is never actually enacted on stage, but is passed on by report several times during the play. This is in keeping with the ideas of report and hearsay which run through the plot. There have been other suggestions why the scene is never enacted. One is that it might detract from the forthcoming 'climax' at Hero's wedding. As you read on, decide whether you think this would have been the case. Can you think of any more reasons?

Act 3, scene 4

Hero, Ursula and Margaret prepare for Hero's wedding that day. Beatrice enters, and the two other women amuse themselves by teasing her about Benedick.

'My cousin's a fool, and thou art another. I'll wear none but this.'

Hero

Fashion

Note, again, how Hero comes into her own amongst her women friends. She jests and banters in a way we never see her do when amongst the men of the play, even lightheartedly responding to the sexual references and innuendo made by Margaret.

Note also that Margaret's and Hero's talk is of fashion and clothing: the ongoing symbols in the play for deception and inconstancy. Whilst this scene is lighthearted in tone, there is some dramatic tension in that the audience have foreknowledge of the events of deception which will spoil Hero's happiness.

'Benedictus! Why Benedictus? You have some moral in this Benedictus!'

In some ways this scene parallells the one in which Benedick's friends tease

Beatrice

him for having 'toothache'. Hero and Margaret know only too well what the cause of her 'illness' is, just as Benedick's friends knew what was ailing him. They take a good-humoured delight in mocking her, however, and Margaret shows her wit by an apparently innocent pun on Benedick's name, saying that it is the only thing that will cure her. Poor Beatrice, like

Benedick, for once has no stinging reply, and the other girls seem to play up to their rare advantage.

Act 3, scene 5

We are now taken back to Dogberry and Verges, who have sought out Leonato and are attempting to convey to him what they have discovered. Leonato is busy with wedding preparations, however, and becomes impatient with them. He finally bids them to deal with the problem themselves and hastily dismisses them.

'Brief, I pray you, for you see it is a busy time with me.'

The plot is complicated, and tension is heightened in several ways here. It is

a

Comic characters

potentially simple matter for Dogberry and Verges to explain the trick to Leonato and have the whole thing cleared up. Leonato's own haste prevents this from happening. The stupidity, pompousness and inarticulacy of the two men make him lose patience, and he turns them away before they finally get round to telling him about Borachio's trick. The

rambling incompetence of Dogberry and Verges is designed to produce suspense for the audience as we wait to see if the pair are able to save Hero from being disgraced. It is ironic that, as well as being comic and foolish figures, Dogberry and Verges are lynchpins to this part of the plot.

Self-test Questions Act Three

Uncover the plot

Delete two of the three alternatives given to find the correct plot. Beware possible misconceptions and muddles.

Hero sends Ursula/Margaret/Ophelia to fetch Beatrice. She tells her to say that Beatrice is being discussed/the dinner is ready/it is midnight, and that she will find them in the orchard/at the fair/inside the house. Hero and Ursula/Margaret/Cleopatra talk loudly of Benedick's love for Beatrice/the weather/Hero's forthcoming wedding in order to trick Beatrice into falling in love with Claudio/Henry/Benedick. The trick works, and Beatrice decides to leave the country/love him back/turn him down.

Benedick's behaviour has changed since he has fallen in love – he is quieter/more tired/easily angered. Don John approaches Claudio/Benedick/Othello and tells him that Hero is in danger/asleep/disloyal. They arrange to watch outside her window/at her door/at the end of her garden in order to see proof. Claudio says that if he sees evidence he will kill her that day/ignore her/shame her in public.

Dogberry and Verges are in charge of the kitchen staff/army/watchmen. They brief them on their duties, telling them to keep a careful eye on Don John's/Banquo's/Leonato's house. The watchmen overhear Borachio/Don John/Macbeth discussing the plan to destroy Rosalind/Benedick's/Claudio's wedding and run off to arrest them. Margaret and Beatrice help Hero to dress for her wedding.

Dogberry and Verges try to tell Leonato/Claudio/Hamlet what they have discovered, but Leonato is impatient/is tired/doesn't care. He tells them to stay on duty/let the prisoners go/examine them on their own.

Who? What? Why? When? Where? How?

1   Where should Ursula tell Beatrice to hide?
2   Who is the 'only man of Italy'?
3   Where does Don Pedro intend to go after Claudio's wedding?
4   What does Benedick say is the reason for his melancholy?
5   What does Don John tell Claudio?
6   Who earns 1,000 Ducats from Don John?
7   What is Beatrice's excuse for her change of mood?
8   Why can't Leonato stop to listen to Dogberry and Verges?
9   Who does Dogberry send Verges to get and why?

Who said that?

1   'She's limed, I warrant you.'
2   'And Benedick, love on;'
3   'I have the toothache.'
4   'She shall be buried with her face upward!'
5   'Is it possible that any villainy should be so dear?'
6   'I am stuffed, cousin, I cannot smell.'
7   'All thy tediousness on me, ah?'
8   'What pace is this that thy tongue keeps?'
9   'We will rather sleep than talk;'
10 'O mischief strangely thwarting!'

Open quotes

Identify the scene; complete the phrase; identify the speaker and the character being spoken to.

1. '…bid her steal into the pleached bower,/where honeysuckles, ripened by the sun…'
2. 'For look where Beatrice, like a lapwing…'
3. 'I know her spirits are as coy and wild/As…'
4. 'And, Benedick, love on…'
5. 'There's no true drop of blood in him to…'
6. 'The world is too good to…'
7. 'Truly, I would not hang a dog by my will, much more…'
8. 'Benedictus! Why Benedictus? You…'
9. '…if I were as tedious as a king, I could…'
10. '…how you may be converted I know not, but methinks…'

Act 4, scene 1

This scene takes place at Hero's wedding. Claudio publicly denounces Hero, and refuses to marry her. He claims that she has deceived him with her innocent appearance, and that really she is no better than a prostitute. Hero speaks out to defend herself, but Claudio, Don Pedro and even her own father are convinced. She faints, and Don Pedro, Don John and Claudio leave. The friar counsels patience and caution and puts forward a plan to announce Hero as dead until they can discover the cause of the misunderstanding. He hopes that time, and grief, will soften Claudio's judgment.

The scene then moves to Benedick and Beatrice, who are left alone after the others have moved away. Beatrice is distraught and Benedick tries to console her. They confess their love for each other, but Beatrice asks Benedick to prove his love by killing his friend Claudio. Benedick is reluctant and taken aback, but eventually agrees.

Note: *This is the climactic scene of the play. The drama reaches its height when Claudio brutally denounces Hero at the church. Tension is sustained by the use of dramatic irony: the audience know how Claudio has been duped, but all other characters — excepting Don John — do not. This scene brings the plot close to tragedy, leading some people to label the play a tragi-comedy: a comedy containing elements of tragedy. Claudio does have many qualities of a tragic hero — he is well respected and highly valued in society and, like Othello or Macbeth, it is an innate weakness that causes him to be susceptible to ill-will and evil.*

The scene centres on the Claudio/Hero plot, but does encompass the second Benedick/Beatrice plot, and Beatrice's challenge to Benedick. In this way, both plots are drawn to their climax.

'No.' *Claudio*

This short, brutal refusal of Claudio to marry Hero is given right at the beginning of the scene and carries much dramatic impact. The misinterpretation of his answer by the other characters builds the tension – we wait for them to understand the meaning of his words. Just as Claudio's outright rejection of Hero is given greater impact by being placed at the start of the scene, the friar is conveniently asked by Leonato to speed up the proceedings so that we can get to the action without unnecessary preamble.

'Give not this rotten orange to your friend; She's but the very semblance of her honour.'

Claudio's language is evocative here. By 'rotten orange' he means that Hero's appearance is as deceptive as fruit rotting inside an apparently perfect skin. It also reminds us, though, of Beatrice's pun on oranges when she was referring to his jealous nature, and this is equally appropriate now. On a more general note, the imagery used often draws on nature, particularly that which reminds us of the Mediterranean setting and climate of the play.

'And seemed I ever otherwise to you?'

In keeping with her characterisation, Hero is slow to speak, listening to Claudio's accusations for a long time before attempting to defend herself. When she does speak, she is typically non-confrontational and unaggressive, leading Claudio to a further outburst.

Hero

'For thee I'll lock up all the gates of love, And on my eyelids shall conjecture hang, To turn all beauty into thoughts of harm, And never shall it more be gracious.'

Claudio acknowledges his gullibility here, although for the wrong reasons, and towards the wrong person. He says that, in future, he will mistrust all that is beautiful to him. Notice that his emphasis is on the visible appearance of things. It is Hero's beauty and innocent appearance which have let him down. This reflects the way that he fell in love – through his eyes.

Claudio

'Death is the fairest cover for her shame That may be wished for.'

Look carefully at Leonato's response to Hero's shame. Once he is (quite quickly) convinced of her guilt, he announces that Hero should be left to die. What do you think of his reaction? It is hard for a modern audience to understand, but do you think he can be justified in his words? What does this say about parental relationships, and the way in which a woman was

Leonato

often regarded by her 'keepers' – first her father and then her husband? How has this changed?

'O, on my soul, my cousin is belied!' Beatrice
'...the practice of it lives in John the Bastard,
Whose spirits toil in frame of villainies.' Benedick

Significantly, it is Beatrice and Benedick who are able to see the truth of the

Self-deception

situation. Beatrice appears to be guided more by her fierce loyalty to her cousin than by reason. Benedick actually suspects the real cause of the problem. Again, despite his 'jester' appearance, we are reminded that Benedick is no fool. Benedick and Beatrice are able to see through the deceptions of others, but they are still blind to their own.

'Come, Lady, die to live; this wedding day
Perhaps is but prolonged; have patience and endure.'

It is the friar who finally resolves the situation. He expresses his faith in Hero,

Deception and disguise

and puts forward his plan of announcing Hero's death – until the 'misprision' is sorted out. He suggests that if Hero's innocence cannot be proven, she should lead a life of religious seclusion.

The friar plays no other real part in the plot and he is not developed in any way. He exists merely as a convenient 'outsider' to guide the troubled family to the best solution.

Unlike the unfortunate friar in *Romeo and Juliet*, his plan has a positive result, although he is not completely correct in his predictions of Claudio's grief.

'I do love nothing in the world so well as you; is not that strange?'

This is a potentially quiet and tender ending to an eventful scene, but the

Beatrice

Benedick

volatile nature of the pair prevent this from being so. Beatrice and Benedick finally confess their love for one another. Ironically, the parting of Claudio and Hero has enabled them to come together. Elizabethan audiences would have been kept amused by their clever word-play on the word 'nothing' (see **Themes and images** section). The potential tender lyricism of this scene is also diverted with Beatrice's challenge to Benedick to 'kill Claudio'.

Here Beatrice asks Benedick to prove his love for her by turning against his friend – an irony discussed previously. Benedick eventually agrees to challenge Claudio. In this part of the scene we see both evidence of his loyalty and devotion to his friends, and his love for Beatrice.

'O God, that I were a man! I would eat his heart in the market-place.'

Note Beatrice's frustration here with her womanhood. Throughout the play

she has not really fitted into the conventional, womanly mould of the period – in many ways she is a heroine ahead of her time. How would Beatrice fare today? Would she be happier, or would she still feel frustrated with her 'passive' feminine role in society?

Beatrice

It is partly Beatrice's position in society that allows her to behave in this unconventional way. Unlike Hero, she has no real relations to answer to, and has to look out for herself in a way that Hero does not. Leonato is her guardian, but his first priority is clearly Hero – Beatrice is not heir to his fortune. She is able to be a 'free spirit', and has not been so dutifully 'trained' in feminine behaviour as her cousin.

How do you see Beatrice's relationship with Benedick? Do you view it as a 'submission' on her part to the convention of married life, and to the authority of a man? Or do you feel that she has merely found a match in Benedick, and remained true to herself? Ask yourself this as you read on. Note, also, the conversation at this part of the scene. How much say does Benedick have in things?

Act 4, scene 2

Dogberry, Verges and the sexton attempt to 'try' Conrade and Borachio.

'Is our whole dissembly appeared?'

Again, this scene is littered with malapropisms, as where Dogberry clearly means 'assembly', not 'dissembly'. Dogberry and Verges are obviously taking great pride in their position of power – and the results are farcical. It is clear to the audience that they are simply acting out a role – one that only they believe in!

Comic characters

Self-test Questions Act Four

Uncover the plot
Delete two of the three alternatives given, to find the correct plot. Beware possible misconceptions and muddles.
Claudio shames Hero at his wedding by ignoring her/refusing to marry her/striking her. Leonato is shocked, but says that if the information is true, it is best she should

see a priest/make amends/be left to die. Hero runs off/is angry/faints. The friar/Antony/Benedick has a plan. He says that they should announce Hero's death/betrothal to another/divorce until they can find the truth/find her a dowry/find a new home for her. Benedick tells Beatrice that he hates her/loves her/will have nothing to do with her and she replies that the feeling is mutual. Beatrice wants him to kill her enemy, Catherine/Claudio/Don John. Benedick asks Horatio/refuses/reluctantly agrees to challenge him.

Dogberry and Verges 'examine' the villains, Conrade and Borachio/Don John/Enobarbus. They take the men to Leonato/Charmian/Claudio to explain the truth. Leonato and his father/brother/cousin Antonio meet Claudio and Don Pedro and they shake hands/quarrel/make up. Benedick challenges Claudio, who finds it hard to take him seriously/is very frightened/tries to run off.

Who? What? Why? When? Where? How?

1   How does Leonato first interpret Claudio's refusal of Hero?
2   Who did Claudio really see at Hero's window?
3   What time was this?
4   Who is the first person to say that Hero is innocent?
5   Who does Benedick guess is behind all the confusion?
6   What is the friar's plan?
7   What does Beatrice command Benedick to do?
8   What does Beatrice say she would do to Claudio if she were a man?
9   Where do Dogberry and Verges intend to take their prisoners after examination?

Who said that?

1   'What men daily do, not knowing what they do!'
2   'And seemed I ever otherwise to you?'
3   'This looks not like a nuptial.'
4   'I talked with no man at that hour, my lord.'
5   'Hath no man's dagger here a point for me?'
6   'Come, lady, die to live…'
7   'Kill Claudio.'
8   'Use it for my love some other way than by swearing by it.'
9   'Thou naughty varlet!'
10 'You are an ass, you are an ass.'

Open quotations

Identify the scene; complete the phrase; identify the speaker and the character being spoken to.

1   'How now! Interjections? Why, then, some be of…'
2   'I never tempted her with word too large, /But, as a brother to a sister, showed…'
3   'You seemed to me as Dian in her orb,/As…'
4   'Come, let us go. These things, come thus to light…'
5   'Death is the fairest cover for her shame/That…'
6   'Dost thou look…'
7   'Sir,sir, be patient./For my part, I am so attired in…'
8   'Being that I flow in…'
9   'I cannot be a man with wishing, therefore…'
10 'You have stayed me in a happy hour; I…'

Act 5, scene 1

Leonato and Antonio confront Claudio and Don Pedro with Hero's supposed 'death'. Benedick arrives and, much to their astonishment, challenges Claudio to a duel. Don Pedro learns that his brother has fled Messina.

Dogberry and company arrive to present their villains to the prince. Borachio confesses. Claudio is overcome with grief, and agrees to Leonato's request that he marries one of his nieces.

'...for, brother, men can counsel and speak comfort to that grief Which they themselves not feel; but, tasting it, Their counsel turns to passion'

Leonato

Leonato gives a long speech at the beginning of this scene, in conversation with his brother Antonio. He tells Antonio not to counsel or comfort him, because it is impossible for him to understand his feelings truly when he is not experiencing his grief, and that, in his position, Antonio would also have no patience.'

Leonato's reluctance to disguise his emotions is consistent with what we have already seen of him. His rash and emotional nature goes some way to explaining his reaction at the church. We see here that he has accepted his daughter's innocence and is ready to avenge her accusers.

'Away! I will not have to do with you!'

Claudio

It is difficult to judge Claudio's reaction to the news of Hero's death. He says very little and we are left to imagine his expression. Is it one of scorn? Of anger? Of sorrow? Do you think he behaves in an appropriate manner? His reserve may very well be through shock, but he seems to bounce back quickly when he meets Benedick later in the scene. He greets him with the jovial phrase 'We had like to have had our two noses snapped off with two old men without teeth' and requests Benedick to cheer them out of their 'melancholy'. Do you find this natural, or in keeping with character? They may have left Hero for dead at the church, but they seem to have very little sympathy for Leonato. Only the prince expresses any sorrow for Hero's death.

'You are a villain; I jest not.'

Notice the response to Benedick's challenge. Claudio and Don Pedro have trouble taking him seriously, and they take the opportunity to tease him about Beatrice. It takes some time before they realise he is in earnest. Claudio correctly guesses that Beatrice is behind all this. Their lighthearted responses contrast well with the 'new' and solemn Benedick, who refuses to rise to their mockery.

'First, I ask thee what they have done; thirdly, I ask what's their offence; sixth and lastly, why they are committed; and, to conclude, what you lay to their charge.'

Don Pedro here cleverly parodies the blundering Dogberry as he tries to find out what crime Conrade and Borachio have committed. It is doubtful that Dogberry notices the mockery in his speech: his stupidity is such that he can transform any insult into a compliment. Dogberry is a good example of self-deception: he is blind to how others perceive him.

'What your wisdoms could not discover, these shallow fools have brought to light.'

Borachio spells out the real irony of the situation. It is the respected, educated and dignified members of society who have been fooled by Don John, whilst the bumbling fools of the town are able to step into the 'hero' role and solve the problem.

'And since you could not be my son-in-law,
Be yet my nephew. My brother hath a daughter,
Almost the copy of my child that's dead.
And she alone is heir to both of us.'

This is a new development for the audience, who know that Hero is not really

dead, but do not know Leonato's plan. The technique is slightly different in this third deception: although the audience may well be able to guess at Leonato's intentions, they are not given this information beforehand, and so there is not the same gap between our knowledge and that of the characters. In this case, we wait with the characters to find out what will happen.

Deception and disguise

Act 5, scene 2

Benedick tries to compose a poem for Beatrice, but finds he cannot do so. He sends Margaret to fetch Beatrice, who asks for information on what happened between him and Claudio. Ursula enters and outlines what has been discovered — that Claudio and Don Pedro had been deceived by Don John, and Hero is proven innocent.

'But I must tell thee plainly, Claudio undergoes my challenge and either I must shortly hear from him, or I will subscribe him a coward.'

Benedick seems rather flippant about his 'challenge' to his friend. Do you think he is confident that he will not keep his appointment? What do you think would have happened if the deception had not been unveiled? Perhaps it is rather convenient for Benedick that it was!

Benedick

50

Act 5, scene 3

Claudio reads his epitaph to Hero at her monument, as requested by Leonato. He is accompanied by Don Pedro and Balthasar and some other mourners.

Note: Notice the poetic quality of the speech in this scene. Claudio tends to talk in verse anyway, but the rhythm and timing of Claudio's and Don Pedro's rhymed speech is exact. It has a lyrical, poignant feel to it which is compounded by the epitaph and by Balthasar's song. This contrasts well with the liveliness of the prose of the scene before. The brevity of this scene also adds to the feel of a 'poetic interlude'. Notice also that Claudio is accompanied by several others. He mourns Hero in the same way as he courted her: formally, and in public.

Act 5, scene 4

This scene takes place on the day of Claudio's marriage – supposedly to Leonato's niece. He is presented with a masked bride and swears to marry her. The bride unmasks, and it is Hero herself. Benedick then asks for Beatrice, and they agree to marry. Right at the end of the scene we learn that Don John has been captured and brought back to Messina.

'...withdraw into a chamber by yourselves, And when I send for you, come hither masked.'

Leonato's plan is slowly unfolding for us here. The women are to present

themselves to Claudio with their faces concealed, so that Hero's identity can be hidden from Claudio until the last moment. There is a feel of ceremony and ritual here, and the mask symbolism brings us back round to the opening act, and the scene of the 'masque'. This symbolism is important for establishing the themes and atmosphere of the play – that of deception, and concealed appearances.

Deception and disguise

'She died, my lord, but whiles her slanders lived.'

The unmasking of Hero completes the third major deception of the play. All

three deceptions have had different motives: the deception of Claudio was in order to destroy a marriage; the deception of Benedick and Beatrice was in order to create a marriage; the deception of Claudio by Leonato was in order to bring about a reconciliation.

Hero

The final deception of Claudio resolves all difficulties. It brings Hero and Claudio back together, and prevents Benedick having to turn against his friend for his lover.

'A miracle! Here's our own hands against our hearts!'

This scene also brings about a resolution to the more lighthearted

Self-deception

Beatrice/Benedick plot. The pair discover that they have been duped, but are happy about the end result. In the end they find that, whilst their witty banter and jokes could conceal their real feelings, their written words have exposed them. It is significant that, while they have been deceived by *spoken* words, it is the visual evidence of written words which unveils the truth. For Beatrice and Benedick, it is the spoken word that has been deceptive – both their own and that of others.

'My lord, your brother John is ta'en in flight, And brought with armed men back to Messina.'

Love and courtship

Finally – the happy ending is crowned with vengeance against the perpetrator of evil, as a messenger arrives to announce that Don John has been captured. All the loose elements are tied up and the play finishes in grand and carefree style with music, dancing and merriment.

Self-test Questions: Act Five

Uncover the plot

Delete two of the three alternatives given to find the correct plot. Beware possible misconceptions and muddles.

Dogberry and Verges go to present the prisoners to Claudio/Leonato/Benedick, but are intercepted by Don Philippe/Don Pedro/Don John. Borachio/Conrade/Banquo tells them the truth, and Claudio is ashamed/devastated/amused. He asks Leonato to chose his revenge/kill him/leave. Leonato says that he must marry his brother's daughter/Hero/Beatrice.

Borachio says that Margaret is alone in her room/innocent of the plot/an accomplice who should be punished. Ursula/Margaret/Hero rushes to Beatrice and Benedick to tell them that the truth has been discovered and that Don John has fled Messina/been punished/killed himself. Claudio reads his epitaph at Hero's tomb which says that she has been killed by Don John/slander/suicide.

Benedick tells Leonato that he wishes to marry Beatrice, and Leonato is surprised/says that he already knows/is delighted.

Claudio thinks he is marrying Hero's cousin/sister/aunt, but is shocked to find that his bride is Hero herself/Margaret/Beatrice. Benedick and Beatrice discover that they have been deceived by their friends/do not like each other/are cousins, but still agree to marry.

Who? What? Why? When? Where? How?

1   Who does Leonato accuse of villainy?

2   What insulting names does Antonio call Claudio and Don Pedro?
3   Who had Claudio and Don Pedro been looking for when they meet Leonato and his brother?
4   To whom do Claudio and Don Pedro attribute Benedick's challenge?
5   Who has left Messina?
6   What does Leonato choose as his 'revenge' against Claudio?
7   Who was 'packed in all this wrong'?
8   Who sings at Hero's funeral?
9   Who brings the good news to Beatrice that her cousin has been saved?

Who said that?
1   'She died, my lord, but whiles her slanders lived.'
2   'I have drunk poison whiles he uttered it.'
3   'If you would know your wronger, look on me.'
4   'God save the foundation!'
5   'Give us the swords; we have bucklers of our own.'
6   'Thou and I are too wise to woo peaceably.'
7   'And I do with an eye of love requite her.'
8   'I'll hold my mind, were she an Ethiope.'
9   'They swore that you were well nigh dead for me.'
10   'How dost, thou, Benedick, the married man?'

Open quotations
Identify the scene; complete the phrase; identify the speaker and the character being spoken to.
1   'He is composed and framed of treachery...'
2   'Art thou the slave that with thy breath...'
3   'Your over kindness doth...'
4   'Only foul words; and...'
5   'I do suffer love indeed...'
6   'Serve God, love me...'
7   'I will live in thy heart, die in thy lap and...' (finish speech)
8   'Now unto thy bones good night!/Yearly...'
9   'Soft and fair, Friar. Which is...'
10   'Prince, thou art sad...'

Self-test Answers Act One

Uncover the plot

Leonato, Governor of Messina, learns of the arrival of Don Pedro, who is Prince of Arragon. He is to arrive with his friend, Claudio. When he arrives, he also brings his brother Don John, and another soldier, Benedick.

Leonato is accompanied by his daughter, Hero, and her cousin Beatrice. Beatrice argues with Benedick and we find out that she has had a long-running feud with him. Leonato welcomes all the visitors, but gives a special welcome to Don John, who is of a reserved nature. Claudio confesses to Benedick that he loves Hero. Benedick is disappointed with his friend and says that he, himself, will never marry. He also says that Beatrice is more attractive than Hero. Don Pedro is sympathetic to Claudio, and tells him that he will woo Hero on his behalf.

Leonato meets his brother, Antonio, who tells him that he has heard that Don Pedro wishes to marry Hero. Don John speaks in private to Conrade and tells him that he wishes to make trouble for his brother. The plan for the marriage is also overheard by Borachio, and Don John resolves to use the information to hurt him.

Who? What? Why? When? Where? How?

1 Claudio
2 He is afraid of her sharp tongue
3 'Signor Montanto'. This is a fencing term, and Beatrice mocks his fighting skills by calling him this
4 Don John
5 Woo Hero for him
6 He wants to know if she is his heir
7 In an alley in his orchard
8 Borachio
9 He has helped to conquer him, and become foremost in his brother's affections
10 Saturn. This is supposed to be the planet of melancholy

Who said that?

1 Leonato
2 Beatrice
3 Don Pedro
4 Beatrice
5 Claudio
6 Benedick
7 Don Pedro
8 Don John
9 Claudio

Open quotes

1 'I pray you, how many hath he killed and eaten in these wars? But how many hath he killed? For indeed, I promised to eat all of his killing.' Beatrice asking the messenger for news of Benedick, Act 1, scene 1
2 'And a good soldier to a lady; but what is he to a lord?' Beatrice talking to the messenger about Benedick, Act 1, scene 1
3 'He is most in the company of the right noble Claudio.' The messenger talking to Beatrice, Act 1, scene 1

4   'If he have caught Benedick, it will cost him a thousand pound 'ere he be cured.' Beatrice talking to the messenger, Act 1, scene 1
5   'You always end with a jade's trick; I know you of old.' Beatrice talking to Benedick, Act 1, scene 1
6   'I dare swear he is no hypocrite, but prays from his heart.' Don Pedro talking to Claudio and Benedick about Leonato's invitation, Act 1, scene 1
7   'As the event stamps them; but they have a good cover; they show well outward.' Antonio telling Leonato about the misheard conversation between Claudio and Don Pedro, Act 1, scene 2
8   'I must be sad when I have cause, and smile at no man's jests eat when I have stomach, and wait for no man's leisure; sleep when I am drowsy, and tend to no man's business; laugh when I am merry, and claw no man in his humour.' Don John explaining his mood to Conrade, Act 1, scene 3
9   'If I had my mouth, I would bite; if I had my liberty, I would do my liking.' Don John talking to Conrade, Act 1, scene 3
10 'To the death, my lord.' Conrade promising allegiance to Don John and his plan, Act 1, scene 3

Self-test Answers Act Two

Uncover the plot

Leonato's family prepare for their party. Leonato reminds Hero that if Don Pedro should ask her to marry him, she should say yes. At the party Don Pedro takes Hero aside and woos her for Claudio. Unfortunately, because of Don John's interference, Claudio believes that Don Pedro has wooed Hero for himself. Beatrice meets Benedick in disguise and the two exchange insults. After Don Pedro has assured Claudio that he has not tricked him, he and Hero arrange to marry on Monday. Claudio had wanted to marry the next day, because he feels that a week is too long too wait. Don Pedro announces that he will try to make a match between Beatrice and Benedick.

Borachio has a plan to help Don John destroy Claudio's marriage. He will ask Margaret, Hero's waiting-woman, to appear with him at Hero's chamber window on the night before the wedding. It will then seem as if Hero has been unfaithful to Claudio.

When Benedick sees Claudio and his friends approaching, he hides in an arbour. His friends pretend not to see him and start talking loudly about Beatrice's love for him. Benedick is shocked, but convinces himself that he must love Beatrice back.

Who? What? Why? When? Where? How?

1   A man halfway between Benedick and Claudio
2   He is going to woo her for Claudio
3   Ursula
4   Benedick
5   Benedick
6   He wants to make Claudio think that Don Pedro has betrayed him
7   A week
8   1,000 ducats
9   Leonato, Claudio, Don Pedro
10 Leonato's involvement. He does not believe he would stoop to such jokes

Who said that?

1 Don Pedro
2 Margaret
3 Benedick
4 Don Pedro
5 Benedick
6 Don Pedro
7 Borachio
8 Don John
9 Benedick
10 Benedick

Open quotes

1 'How tartly that gentleman looks! I can never see him but I am heartburned an hour after.' Beatrice talking to Leonato and Antonio about Don John, Act 2, scene 1

2 '...let him be a handsome fellow, or else make another curtsy and say, "Father, as it please me"'. Beatrice talking to Hero about her choice of husband, Act 2, scene 1

3 'If the prince do solicit you in that kind, you know your answer.' Leonato telling Hero to accept the prince, Act 2, scene 1

4 'Thus answer I in name of Benedick/but here these ill news with the ears of Claudio.' Claudio after being tricked by Don John into thinking Don Pedro has betrayed him, Act 2, scene 1

5 'O, she misused me past the endurance of a block.' Benedick talking to Don Pedro about Beatrice's insults to him, Act 2, scene 1

6 'I cannot endure my lady tongue.' Benedick talking to Don Pedro about Beatrice, Act 2, scene 1

7 'Indeed, my lord, he lent it me awhile and I gave him use for it.' Beatrice talking to Don Pedro about how she once gave her heart to Benedick, Act 2, scene 1

8 '...she hath often dreamt of unhappiness and waked herself with laughing.' Leonato talking to Don Pedro about Beatrice, Act 2, scene 1

9 'Proof enough to misuse the Prince, to vex Claudio to undo Hero and kill Leonato.' Borachio talking to Don John about his plan to destroy the marriage, Act 2, scene 2

10 'I will, in the interim, undertake one of Hercules' labours; which is, to bring Signor Benedick and Lady Beatrice into a mountain of affection th'one with th'other.' Don Pedro explaining his plan to his friends, Act 2, scene 1

Self-test Answers Act Three

Uncover the plot

Hero sends Margaret to fetch Beatrice. She tells her to say that Beatrice is being discussed, and that she will find them in the orchard. Hero and Margaret talk loudly of Benedick's love for Beatrice, in order to trick Beatrice into falling in love with Benedick. The trick works, and Beatrice decides to love him back.

Benedick's behaviour has changed since he has fallen in love – he is quieter. Don John approaches Claudio and tells him that Hero is disloyal. They arrange to watch outside her window in order to see proof. Claudio says that if he sees evidence he will shame her in public.

Dogberry and Verges are in charge of the watchmen. They brief them on their duties, telling them to keep a careful eye on Leonato's house. The watchmen over-hear Borachio discussing the plan to destroy Claudio's wedding and run off to arrest them. Margaret and Beatrice help Hero to dress for her wedding.

Dogberry and Verges try to tell Leonato what they have discovered, but Leonato is impatient. He tells them to examine them on their own.

Who? What? Why? When? Where? How?

1 In 'the pleached bower' of honeysuckles
2 Benedick
3 Arragon
4 Toothache
5 That Hero has been disloyal
6 Borachio
7 She has a cold
8 He has to get to the wedding
9 Francis Seacoal, because he can write

Who said that?

1 Ursula
2 Beatrice
3 Benedick
4 Don Pedro
5 Conrade
6 Beatrice
7 Leonato
8 Beatrice
9 A watchman
10 Claudio

Open quotes

1 '…bid her steal into the pleached bower,/Where honeysuckles, ripened by the sun/Forbid the sun to enter-like favourite,/Made proud by princes, that advance their pride/Against that power that bred it.' Hero to Margaret about the plan to make Beatrice fall in love, Act 3, scene 1
2 'For look where Beatrice, like a lapwing, runs/close by the ground, to hear our conference.' Hero to Margaret, Act 3, scene 1
3 'I know her spirits are as coy and wild as/As haggards of the rock.' Hero to Ursula about Beatrice, Act 3, scene 1
4 'And, Benedick, love on; I will requite thee,/Taming my wild heart to thy loving hand.' Beatrice on hearing that Benedick loves her, Act 3, scene 1.
5 'There's no true drop of blood in him to be truly touched with love; if he be sad, he wants money.' Don Pedro to Claudio about Benedick, Act 3, scene 2
6 'The world is too good to paint out her wickedness.' Don John to Claudio about Hero's supposed disloyalty, Act 3, scene 2
7 'Truly, I would not hang a dog by my will, much more a man who hath any honesty in him.' Dogberry to Verges whilst instructing the watch, Act 3, scene 3
8 'Benedictus! Why Benedictus? You have some moral in this Benedictus!' Beatrice to Margaret when Margaret is teasing her about her love for Benedick, Act 3, scene 4
9 '… if I were as tedious as a king, I could find it in my heart to bestow it all of your worship.' Dogberry in an attempt to explain his discovery to Leonato, Act 3, scene 5
10 '… how you may be converted I know not, but methinks you look with your eyes as other women do.' Margaret to Beatrice, Act 3, scene 4

Self Test Answers Act Four

Uncover The Plot:

Claudio shames Hero at his wedding by refusing to marry her. Leonato is shocked, but says that, if the information is true, it is best she should be left to die. Hero faints. The friar has a plan. He says that they should announce Hero's death until they can find the truth. Benedick tells Beatrice that he loves her and she replies that the feeling is mutual. Beatrice wants him to kill her enemy, Claudio. Benedick reluctantly agrees to challenge him.

Dogberry and Verges 'try' the villains, Conrade and Borachio. They take the men to Leonato to explain the truth. Leonato and his brother Antonio meet Claudio and Don Pedro and they quarrel. Benedick challenges Claudio, who finds it hard to take him seriously.

Who? What? Why? When? Where? How?

1 He thinks it is a joke
2 Margaret and Borachio
3 Between twelve and one o'clock
4 Beatrice
5 Don John
6 To say that Hero is dead until the truth is discovered
7 Kill Claudio
8 Eat his heart in the market-place
9 To Leonato's house

Who said that?

1 Claudio
2 Hero
3 Benedick
4 Hero
5 Leonato
6 The friar
7 Beatrice
8 Beatrice
9 Dogberry
10 Conrade

Open quotes

1 'How now! Interjections? Why, then, some be of laughing!' Benedick at Claudio's wedding, Act 4, scene 1
2 'I never tempted her with word too large,/But as a brother to a sister,/showed/Bashful sincerity and comely love.' Claudio to Leonato on being asked if he had taken Hero's virginity, Act 4, scene 1
3 'You seemed to me as Dian in her orb,/As chaste as the bud ere it be blown.' Claudio to Hero, Act 4, scene 1
4 'Come, let us go. These things, come thus to light,/Smother her spirits up. Don John to Don Pedro and Leonato, about Hero's faint, Act 4, scene 1
5 'Death is the fairest cover for her shame/That can be wished for.' Leonato talking about Hero, Act 4, scene 1
6 'Dost thou look up?' Leonato speaking to Hero about her shame, Act 4, scene 1
7 'Sir, sir be patient./For my part, I am so attired in wonder,/I know not what to say.' Benedick to Leonato Act 4, scene 1

8   'Being that I flow in grief,/The smallest twine may lead me.' Leonato's response to Benedick's advice to do as the friar says, Act 4, scene 1

9   'I cannot be a man with wishing, therefore I will die a woman with grieving.' Beatrice to Benedick about her wish to avenge her cousin, Act 4, scene 1

10   'You have stayed me in a happy hour; I was about to protest I loved you.' Beatrice to Benedick on hearing that he loves her, Act 4, scene 1

Self-test Answers Act Five

Uncover the plot

Dogberry and Verges go to present the prisoners to Leonato, but are intercepted by Don Pedro. Borachio tells them the truth, and Claudio is devastated. He asks Leonato to choose his revenge. Leonato says he must marry his brother's daughter. Borachio says that Margaret is innocent of the plot. Ursula rushes to Beatrice and Benedick to tell them that the truth has been discovered and that Don John has fled Messina. Claudio reads his epitaph at Hero's tomb which says that she has been killed by slander.

Benedick tells Leonato that he wishes to marry Beatrice, and Leonato is surprised. Claudio thinks he is marrying Hero's cousin, but is shocked to find that his bride is Hero herself. Benedick and Beatrice discover that they have been deceived by their friends, but still agree to marry.

Who? What? Why? When? Where? How?

1   Claudio
2   Boys, apes, braggarts, Jacks, milksops
3   Benedick
4   Beatrice
5   Don John
6   He must marry his brother's daughter (not Beatrice, though)
7   Margaret
8   Balthasar
9   Ursula

Who said that?

1   Leonato
2   Claudio
3   Borachio
4   Dogberry
5   Margaret
6   Benedick
7   Benedick
8   Claudio
9   Beatrice
10   Don Pedro

Open quotes

1   'He is composed and framed of treachery,/And fled he is upon this villainy.' Don Pedro to Claudio about his brother, Act 5, scene 1

2   'Art thou the slave that with thy breath hast killed/Mine innocent child?' Leonato asking Borachio about his part in the plot, Act 5, scene 1

3   'Your over kindness doth wring tears from me.' Claudio to Leonato on learning of his 'punishment', Act 5, scene 1

4 'Only foul words; and thereupon I will kiss thee.' Benedick to Beatrice in answer to her question about the challenge to Claudio, Act 5, scene 2

5 'I do suffer love indeed, for I love thee against my will.' Benedick to Beatrice, Act 5, scene 2

6 'Serve God, love me, and mend.' Benedick to Beatrice, Act 5, scene 2

7 'I will live in thy heart, die in thy lap and be buried in thy eyes; and moreover, I will go with thee to thy uncle's.' Benedick to Beatrice on hearing the good news about Hero, Act 5, scene 2

8 'Now unto thy bones good night!/Yearly will I do this rite.' Claudio at Hero's tomb, Act 5, scene 3

9 'Soft and fair, Friar. Which is Beatrice?' Benedick asking for Beatrice to step forward so that he can propose, Act 5, scene 4

10 'Prince, thou art sad; get thee a wife, get thee a wife.' Benedick to the prince when all has been resolved, Act 5, scene 4

◼ Writing an examination essay

Take the following to heart

- *Carefully study each of the questions set on a particular text* Make sure you understand what they are asking for so that you select the one you know most about.
- *Answer the question* Obvious, isn't it? But bitter experience shows that many students fail because they do not actually answer the question that has been set.
- *Answer all the question* Again, obvious, but so many students spend all their time answering just part of a question and ignoring the rest. This prevents you gaining marks for the parts left out.

The question

1 Read and understand every word of it. If it asks you to compare (the similarities) and/or contrast (the differences) between characters or events, then that is what you must do.
2 Underline all the key words and phrases that mention characters, events and themes, and all instructions as to what to do, e.g. compare, contrast, outline, comment, give an account, write about, show how/what/where.
3 Now write a short list of the things you have to do, one item under the other. A typical question will only have between two and five items at most for you to cope with.

Planning your answer

1 Look at each of the points you have identified from the question. Think about what you are going to say about each. Much of it will be pretty obvious, but if you think of any good ideas, jot them down before you forget them.
2 Decide in what order you are going to deal with the question's major points. Number them in sequence.
3 So far you have done some concentrated, thoughtful reading and written down maybe fifteen to twenty words. You know roughly what you are going to say in response to the question and in what order – if you do not, you have time to give serious thought to trying one of the other questions.

Putting pen to paper

The first sentences are important. Try to summarise your response to the question so the examiner has some idea of how you are going to approach it. Do not say 'I am going to write about the character of Macbeth and show how evil he was' but instead write 'Macbeth was a weak-willed, vicious traitor. Totally dominated by his "fiend-like queen", he deserved the epitaph "this dead butcher" – or did he?' Jump straight into the essay, do not nibble at its extremities for a page and a half. High marks will be gained by the candidate who can show he or she has a mind engaged with the text. Your personal response is rewarded – provided you are answering the question!

As you write your essay *constantly refer back to your list of points* and make sure you are actually responding to them.

How long should it be?

There is no 'correct' length. What you must do is answer the question set, fully and sensitively, in the time allowed. Allocate time to each question according to the percentage of marks awarded for it.

How much quotation or paraphrase?

Use only that which is relevant and contributes to the quality and clarity of your answer. Padding is a waste of your time and gains not a single mark.